THE VALIANT

THE VALIANT

*Chronicles of
Entrepreneurs*

CA. MOFFAT NGALANDE

MiReads

Contents

Dedication — vi
Valiant — vii
Chivalry — ix
Foreword — xi

1 Stain Singo — 1

2 Newton Kambala — 18

3 Rachel Sibande — 29

4 Mark Katsonga — 39

5 Mike Mlombwa — 55

6 Dr. Thom Mpinganjira — 74

7 Napoleon Dzombe — 90

8 Lilly Alfonso — 104

9 Ngabaghila Chatata — 116

10 Dingase Tewete — 128

11 Towera Jalakasi — 139

12 Maya Nkoloma — 149

About The Author — 160

Sean and Aretha,

"I love you to the moon and back!
"Thank you for your smiles, laughs and purpose you bring"

Valiant

Valiance

Brave

Daring

Courageous

Audacious

Audacity

Ambitious

Fearless

Unrelenting

Unflinching

Chivalry

I would like to thank each of the entrepreneurs featured in this book for your kindness and demonstration of true chivalry.

Chivalry is simply an honorable and polite way of behaving and I have seen this in all of you. You opened your doors when you did not have to, and told your stories when you did not need to. The telling of your stories or lack thereof, will not have made you any better, or richer, or worse off.

The 4th and 5th Commandments of the Chivalric code say

"Thou shalt love the country in which though wast born"
and
"though shalt not recoil before thine enemy"

And the sharing of your story is a demonstration of patriotism for Mother Malawi and demonstrates your desire to inspire others with lessons and values needed to succeed in business for the betterment of our nation.

In the midst of various forms of adversity, you chose to press on and not recoil before your merciless enemy in all its forms and guises.

You simply chose to behave honorably and politely. And for your noble display of humility and chivalry... I say thank you, thank you kindly, for gracing me with an audience, and our readers with such inspirational stories.

Foreword

I grew up in a rural area in the Nkhamanga 'Kingdom' near Bolero in Rumphi district, where my parents, now retired, were primary school teachers. One of the schools they taught at, Jumbi F. P. School was right on the boundary with Nyika National Park. As young boys, we occasionally crossed the boundary in search of wild birds and, at times, wild animals for meat!

The first time my parents had electricity and running water in their home was when they relocated to Ekwendeni in 1996, when my father took on early retirement due to his ailing health . That was just a year before I went to university to study Electrical Engineering at the, then, Malawi Polytechnic and now The Malawi University of Business and Applied Sciences (MUBAS). A year later, Moffat Ngalande joined us at MUBAS and so, I have known him for more than two decades as a very smart accountant and auditor. A man gifted with introspect and reflection on issues.

Moffat has been reflecting on his own, as well as the achievements of others – some well-known to the public and others not so revealed. He has been wise to collect together amazing stories of some of the great successful people around us so that we can not only get inspired by them but also, we can learn how to excel in life.

What is even better, is that most of the stories include not just the vision they have or had, or the amount of determination they possess, but also, the challenges they faced and how they conquered them. As it is always said, you do not need to reinvent the wheel. Here is a unique chance for you and I, to avoid the many hurdles awaiting us on this life's amazing journey, by learning from the great personalities in our midst.

I saw no electricity or running water for 18 years in our house but ended up with a PhD from Oxford University which is often ranked a top 5 university in the world, and reached levels of CEO, having worked abroad including in Europe. To achieve this transformative journey, I keep following stories of people who achieved a lot in life, from humble beginnings. And, I keep learning. I am always keen to understand how those ahead of me did it. I keep learning how they did well, the mistakes they made and how they dealt with hurdles and challenges along the way.

Moffat's book makes this easier for me because I do not need to meet all these amazing people. I just need to grab a copy of his book and read it, then I have all the stories. Waste no time too, as time stands still for no one! Grab his book, read it with a reflective mind, like does the author, and you will be good.

Remember, that above all, you need to draw up your own action plan arising from the great lessons contained in this great book. Good luck!

Eng. Dr. Matthews Mtumbuka

I

Stain Singo

"The employee who believed he could!"

Mr. Stain Singo is the Founder and Chief Executive Officer of Smile Life Insurance Limited.

Smile Life is the first wholly Malawian-owned life insurance company licensed by the Reserve Bank of Malawi (RBM).

FAST FACTS

Date of Birth 10th October 1956, Blantyre Malawi
Company Smile Life insurance Limited. Founded on 1ˢᵗ April 2009.

The company offers life insurance such as Group Life Insurance Cover, Group Funeral Insurance Cover for employees, Group Credit Insurance Covers, Individual and Family Funeral Insurance Covers.

Achievements The Company received an excellence award for service delivery in funeral schemes in Malawi in the year 2015
Countries Malawi
Financial Information

Total income : K1.2 bn,
post tax profits K24 omn
Total assets K2 bn

Information is an approximation for the year ended 31 December 2021

Education

M.C.E. – Malawi – 1975

G.C.E. – Economics Grade 'A' O Level – 1977

Zomba Catholic Secondary School, MSCE, 1979

Professional Qualifications:

- Associate of Chartered Insurance Institute – ACII – U.K. 1985
- Life Assurance Salesman Certificate – Chartered Insurance   Institute – U.K. 1987
- Chartered Insurer – U.K. – 1995

Stain's Background

Stain Singo is my name, I was born on 10 October 1956 in Nkhatabay at a place called Saint Maria Goreti in a Catholic mission hospital. Nkhatabay did not have a proper government district hospital at the time and the mission hospital is now converted into an orphanage. My father was working in the Malawi Police Force and was transferred a lot from duty station to duty station, hence I and my siblings were born in various districts so that I was born in Nkhatabay, my brother in Karonga, my sister in Mzimba and my much younger brother, who used to play in the Malawi national football team in the early 90's was born in Rumphi.

So most of my earlier years were spent in the northern region were we lived for about 10 years. When my father was transferred back to the southern region, just before the independence of Malawi from British colonial rule, the only language I could speak fluently was Tumbuka, a language from the northern part of Malawi.

This is because in those days education in the north was delivered only in Tumbuka. We had Tumbuka books and all the teaching was in Tumbuka and so I was so fluent in Tumbuka to the extent that I was no longer considered to be from anywhere else.

Interestingly though, I am from Lunzu, which is just 20km from Blantyre. But my parents, on my mother's side, came from a place called Khwisa, which is now Balaka, the area was originally under Senior Traditional Authority (STA) Kwataine of Ntcheu but is now under STA Makwangwala. In the olden days they trekked to Blantyre. This happened because they used to sell cattle to the white missionaries that were in the Blantyre Mission which is roughly a 150km distance. And as they travelled down to Blantyre, they used to see very nice places more beautiful that their original home and they decided to ask for land in Blantyre and so they relocated to an area called Ntenjera in Lunzu. However, this was a typical southern region Yao (tribe) village while my parents were typically Ngoni people who had a lot of liberties for eating meats as opposed to the Yao.

So naturally, my parents ate all sorts of foods which were offensive to the Yao for cultural and religious reasons. We ate meats of mbewa and Nkhumba (mice and pork) for example which was not compatible with the Yao traditions. Eventually the Chief approached them and asked them to move out of the village to an outer part of his kingdom. He told them to settle there and gave them the liberty to name their village. So my grandparents called it Khwisa Village because that was the name of their original home in Balaka, where they were coming from. Therefore, I am proud to say that we are village headmen because we are the people who actually started the village.

But enough about my history... When I trace my roots, the entrepreneurial spirit was still there in my great grandparents as they traded in cattle and this spirit has shown itself again in my life story which is about to unfold.

As explained, I did most of my primary school education in various districts of the country because of the nature of my father's job as a police man who used to be transferred from one district to another, but I wrote my standard eight examinations at Henry Henderson Institute (HHI) primary school, which was a mission school. When I completed grade 8, which was the last class in primary school, and was waiting for results of secondary school selection, my father had just retired and had bought himself a new Mazda 1-ton pickup truck because he wanted to be in the fish selling business. This business was, at the time, quite popular and profitable as many would buy fish from the lakeshore areas like Mangochi and resale it in town. I used to help my father in selling the fish and would also go with him to Mangochi, so this was my first experience in business. I was doing this with my brother who was already at HHI Secondary school in Form 2. However due to my young age I really did not have any real interest in money. So I think my father preferred doing his business with me because I really did not have much use for his money other than buying a few bottles of Fanta for my friends, without any real risk of significant loss and wastage.

However, we were brought up in the true Ngoni culture of herding cattle despite our educational achievements. My mother had cattle which we would herd during the holidays and when I was in Form 1 at HHI Secondary school, over the weekends I could go and herd the cattle and on Monday I would be back in class with my fellow students without them knowing that I had spent the week-end brushing shoulders with other herd men, some of whom had never been to school at all.

Sometimes in the mornings before going to school, our parents would take us to the maize gardens and we would till the gardens and then go to school afterwards, they would wake us up early in the morning around 4 am, and then around 6 am go back home where we would find porridge already prepared for us. They would take us to school in a van to HHI Primary School and my brother to secondary school. I did not know that they were preparing me for the future and that's how we grew up.

I was later selected to HHI secondary school where I joined my brother up to form four when I wrote my Malawi School Certificate of Education Exams (MSCE). However, the industrious spirit of waking up early and working was still there since growing up with cattle herders is a tough life because it's not easy, it's really survival of the fittest and this makes you become a different person, so that's the background I had.

My working experience

After I finished my secondary school in 1975, I got a job in the same year with the National Insurance Company of Malawi Limited ("NICO"). Firstly, I enrolled for a General Certificate of Education in Economics examination in 1977 which I passed with grade A, and I did this course from 1978 to 1979.

I was still with NICO at the time and had come to the job with the inherent strengths and benefits of my hardworking spirit. And because of this, my bosses saw potential in me and encouraged me to study insurance as a profession. Insurance is generally a very challenging course to study because it is very statistical and mathematical in nature. I was able to pass my exam every year at each and every sitting. I studied an "Introduction to Insurance" course which had three subjects and you were required to pass all the three subjects within three years in order to progress to the Advanced Diploma level.

These first modules of insurance included, introduction to insurance comprising English law, English and principles of insurance which were to be passed in 3 years in order to progress to the advanced diploma stage. I and my colleague Chris Kapanga managed to pass them in only 2 years. So both Chris and I were allowed to proceed to the advanced diploma stage.

I embarked on the Advanced Diploma which had ten subjects in 1980. In 1984 I was sent to the College of Insurance in India and qualified in 1985 with a distinction in quantitative methods as applied to Insurance. My discipline of waking up early in the morning to work, helped me to study seriously even while working throughout my schooling journey until I was sent to college.

By the time we were qualifying there were only 4 chartered Malawian insurers in the country and the rest were all whites. And in 1985 there were three of us who qualified, namely myself, Chris Kapanga and Mr. Felix Mlusu.

As far as my work was concerned, I was getting promoted almost every year. And, as alluded to earlier, I was sent to a College of Insurance in India in 1984 and at the time I had 3 or 4 subjects remaining to complete my diploma. As I was completing my diploma, I was sent to Cape Town in South Africa on attachment with some actuaries because my final module had to do with actuarial studies called "quantitative methods as applied to insurance". This was a very difficult subject. It was so mathematical, and the first 2 pages were full of formulas to be used during study. I remember our colleagues from the Malawi Polytechnic used to tell us that "this subject is too difficult." "We have done it in the University of Malawi and failed and there is no way you can pass this subject".

And true to the challenging nature of the subject, I failed it on my first attempt. So, I decided to leave this subject until the end of the course. This allowed me to pass the other subjects and only remain with quantitative methods. I was then very focused on this subject, eating and breathing it each and every day! I had to set my priorities right, I therefore abandoned everything else and concentrated on studying. At that time, I was an ardent supporter of the Mighty Wanderers, but I had to abandon all that and focus on quantitative methods. And indeed, my efforts paid off, because I passed it with distinction and was the first Malawian to pass it with distinction. Even my college tutors wrote me and asked how a person from Africa can pass this subject with distinction because this subject is too difficult.

And true to their word, they withdrew the subject within 2 years because students were complaining that it is too difficult. They then split the topics and included them in various other modules to ensure that the essentials were still covered, including actuarial science, statistics etc. I actually got an award for passing with distinction.

This helped me to further do well in my career because I was then promoted to Senior Manager of Pensions in the life and insurance company of NICO. At the time the general manager was white and was returning to his home and they therefore planned to recruit Malawians. The current general manager called me and said I would like to put you in the general insurance company because that's where you have a higher chance of success in this company. So I went to the general insurance section and headed the claims section of the business. I was only there for 2 years because my boss who was in the life and pension company retired early. The board decided to retire him and bring me back. I was therefore called back to head the company and I became the first Malawian General Manager (GM) of NICO Life.

I was GM for the company for almost 10 years and during that time I was sent to attend a good number of courses across several countries including Malta, United Kingdom, South Africa America- Columbia University where I studied change management and visited several other countries.

The genesis of Smile Life

Now for the beginning of Smile Life! I believe it was in 2007 when NICO sent me to Cape Town South Africa for a workshop that was organised by Hannover Re. The course was called "Business Game". This workshop was about "role playing" how to run an insurance company not from an employee's point of view but an investors point of view or running the business as a shareholder or owner.

We were given several scenarios with good and bad end results with the aim of coaching you on how to actually run an insurance company. This course, planted something within me, and that's when I said to myself "maybe I should start thinking of owning an insurance company". A spark was kindled in my heart which later became a full-blown fire!

I discussed this with my then fiancé Hilda who is now my wife. She looked favourably on the idea because also owing to the fact that she had just returned from completing her MBA in Scotland and part of her studies included studies like entrepreneurship.

"I think you can do it" she said and cheered me on.

I believe that God has got his own ways of preparing somebody for certain things in future, because there are certain things that happen over which you do not have control, but they are controlled by God for a purpose. I had lost my first wife in 2003, this was a painful event not only for me but also for my children but God's word is true that He makes all things work together for good because in even such a painful event like the loss of my spouse God strengthened me. And at the lowest point in my life, God sent me Hilda at an appropriate time in life because she was so instrumental in the formation of Smile Life and she pushed me forward and cheered me on to, not only leave NICO, but also to establish a new company from scratch.

She was not fearful of the fact that I was among the 5 most highly paid Malawians in NICO at that time and most people thought I was crazy to leave all the company benefits and perks.

"he is someone we envy being in his position, and he is now leaving!" they would say! My perks included a good pay and travel, children's school fees at St. Andrews International High School, a prestigious primary school, was fully paid for, company vehicles were fully serviced by the company and I had other similar benefits. In fact, my colleagues were calling each other saying Stain has gone insane, and they would call me asking me why I am leaving NICO.

I strongly believe that Hilda came at a right time in my life to propel me in this direction of business because I did not have my first wife to encourage me and cheer me on, but she helped by playing this important role of companion and friend when I was taking on a big challenge alone. But indeed with her I wasn't alone.

So even though we went through a painful experience with the loss of my wife in 2003, all things worked together in the end so that all was not lost but something good could still happen through it all. So sometimes you really need inspiration and above all a bigger power beyond you and I knew it was God, and of course with encouragement from my darling Hilda and others that walked with me.

My motivation was that at the time I took over NICO Life, the assets under management were under K10 billion with annual premiums of below K500m but the time I am leaving in late 2022, the company had assets in excess of K20 billion with annual premiums in excess of K1 billion, and with much more significant assets owned by the company. and in present day, you very well know that its a much bigger company.

When I reflect on these things, I realise that I could not, indeed, have done it on my own and, I had a passion for insurance, because I had not worked in any other field apart from insurance. Looking back at this, I realise, time and again, that it is usually other people who see potential in us and not ourselves. We are usually held back by the fear of failure and other things.

I knew that this was a big task and realised that I could not just do it on my own but will need help from some friends. So I started discussing this with some trusted colleagues in the company. One of them was Beatrice Mangwana, I employed her in NICO and she had just qualified, as an insurer and immediately she proceeded with her MBA, so I took note of her achievements and thought "I think this lady has a passion for insurance, is focused and self-driven" and I would need people like her if I am going to go into this task because it is not an easy task. I approached her and she said, "let me think about it". She later came back and confirmed that "ok I will support you I think I can do it".

Then I said, "I also need somebody in addition to you so that there can be 3 of us." And I spoke to Arnold Nyirenda who was our marketing manager in NICO life at that time. I told him that I will need a marketer and he said "let's talk about it". After our discussion he said "let me think about it" and was honestly, more difficult than Beatrice because he took quite some convincing before I prevailed and he finally agreed.

But agree he did! And that was the most important thing. The three of us agreed that we still needed other people, who were well known and had achieved something in society and that's when I approached Mr. Kambalame, who was the former General Manager of Operations at the Reserve Bank of Malawi. I had interacted with him on the board of Associated Pensions Trust Limited where he was the board chair. And he said if it's you then I am prepared to put in my money. And I said "ahh very good! I needed you to be on board" and he was indeed very instrumental due to his connections and experience with the Reserve Bank.

In fact if he had not been with us I do not know if we would have made the strides we have made so far because he was instrumental in negotiations with the central bank and most of the senior people including the then governor had very high respect for him because he had actually employed some of them into the central bank.

I also approached George Naphambo and then Mr. Jolly Nkhonjera and so we started Smile Life in April 2009 and in that year alone we wrote a premium of K22 million. As of December 2015, after 6 years and 9 months we are closing with K672 million! A growth rate of 3055% In fact the actuarial experts state that the gestation period for an insurance company is 8 to 10 years and so this business is not a short term investment where you can invest today and get a dividend tomorrow, and in fact some of the investors indeed expected short term dividend which is something we had to deal with by explaining to them the nature of the insurance business.

The good thing is that almost 13 years later we are still making strides. We set an ambitious target of writing a premium of at least 1 billion if we could and we recently passed that threshold in 2020. But now we quickly want to pass the K2bn mark with our second major milestone being the K5bn mark. We have always set very ambitious targets considering the state of our economy, but it's good to be ambitious because if you miss an ambitious target you still end up achieving significant growth.

Challenges along the way

We, however, experienced a number of challenges, firstly the nature of our business is not like the restaurant business whose demand can rise just by the good smell of food noticed by passers-by or because of the sign that says "open". In this economic economic environment demand is very difficult to generate, more so because of the dominant players that were already there in the market. Initially we had 3 main players namely Nico Life, Old Mutual, and Vanguard. At first, they dismissed us because they thought these guys are too small. In the first year we wrote K22 million in 2009, then jumped to K79 million in 2010 and then to K279 million in 2011 and now we are at much higher levels. That's when they started waking up that there is a new player in the market.

Our growth meant their loss of business especially because the Malawi market is small with minimal new investment. And when companies lose business, they basically have to explain the reasons to their boards and that's when we were considered a force to be reckoned with, but in retaliation, price wars actually began. The larger companies could afford to slash their prices because they have accumulated a lot of reserves over the years.

However, we excelled because our approach was to "make insurance affordable" and this even became our slogan. In fact, when I was in NICO, some of the foreign board members and shareholders said "how can you achieve this much growth without stealing from people? This is theft, and the customers must be suffering."

And they said there must be something wrong with your pricing. This was more so because at that time the life insurance business was making huge profits compared to the general insurance business. So we decided to develop an affordable pricing structure which also covers our risk while remaining in business.

Another challenge is the fact that insurance policies have specific dates at which they are renewed which is mostly from January to March of each year. And by the time we started in April, we had essentially "missed" the opportunity to write a bulk of the new business.

We also had to deal with the challenge of gaining the confidence of our customers. We were told in our faces that,

"When you were with NICO you achieved great things, but it was mainly because you were with an established company with huge assets and the ability to pay claims".

And some our friends in high places who were willing to assist us, would say

"Stain I want to assist you but if I give you business and you fail to pay a claim, I will be answerable to the board (of directors) and put my job at risk, so why should I risk my job for you?"

So that was the biggest challenge in the early years. That's what I call the "wait and see" approach. This fear in the market was reinforced by the fact that there were many companies in the market that had gone bust after 2 to 3 years of operations for various reasons. But normally it takes time of about 4 or 5 years for people to trust you and to establish yourself as a trusted company in the market.

But surprisingly, there were some customers who trusted us right from the word go and these were companies like First Merchant Bank Limited (now First Capital Bank Ltd). This was mainly due to the good service we had given them in the past at NICO and since they had confidence in us they really helped by supporting us with their business.

Another challenge is that Malawians have been made to believe that "foreign is best" and that local businesses cannot offer the same quality of service that NICO or Old Mutual offer especially if it is such a technical field like insurance.

Another thing we did was to focus on is customer service, because we said

"you know what, when a person gets insurance, he gets it for the rainy day and he needs it immediately and it's not for us to take away the umbrella in the rain!"

So we studied how long it takes for these claims to be paid and estimated a period of even 6 months to 1 year according to the prevailing industry practice. We committed ourselves to a higher standard and we said "at Smile life no claim will ever go beyond 30 days'.

We believed that if we did that, word would spread in the market and we would be the preferred insurer". We would pay them as soon as we get all the necessary documentation and also, we would ensure that our clients know what to expect from us. We would explain to them in detail regarding the claim procedure, required documentation and even give them claim forms to keep for use in the event of a claim ...

Word quickly spread around and in our adverts we usually referred to our existing customers as points of reference for anyone who was considering coming to us.

Another challenge was the culture in Malawi towards the business of life insurance. Malawians do not really plan for death and normally react in the moment, and mostly, we bank on financial support from our employers. To talk of funeral planning was actually a taboo in Malawi but we dealt with this by being proactive and being the first company in Malawi to introduce funeral cover.

We marketed the product to break the cultural taboo by focusing on the benefits of planning for such unfortunate events and now people are buying our products. We even put in place measures including standby procedures and strategic market alliances to ensure that our customers are served speedily when a death occurs.

Other companies shortly followed suit by introducing other types of cover such as those offered by some telecommunications and banking companies. We set such a really good pace that we received an excellence award for service delivery in funeral schemes in Malawi in the year 2015. We were in first place while TNM Limited followed our lead and were in second place and the third was NICO.

The enactment of the Pensions Act 2010 has meant that employers are now required, by law, in section 15 of the Act, to provide group life insurance cover for their employees that covers at least the annual salary of the employee. This regulation has boosted the pension business in Malawi and the tendency has been to have both pension and group life policies being done by the same company, but now the law has allowed for these to be separated and it actually increases the efficiency of payment where companies are competing on quality of service.

Another challenge that exists in insurance is that some risks may be very large to the extent that even the insurer himself needs to be insured by another insurer. So we manage this problem by getting what is called "re-insurance" which is essentially "insurance for the insurer". Smile life is re-insured by Hannover-Re and Munich-Re who are very big and well-established re-insurers. This gives us a lot of stability and confidence that there is no risk that is too large for us to cover.

We also use actuaries who are experts at assessing the level of risk in every policy through statistical methods. They help you to determine the right pricing and rates for insurance premiums that enable you to adequately cover your risk, we were using Alexander Forbes of East Africa, and recently use Zamara, all based in Kenya as our Actuaries.

Insurance fraud has also been another interesting challenge for us because there are Malawians who are bent on simply defrauding insurance companies. They come up with ways of how to defraud companies but fortunately this type of fraud in life insurance is not as high as it is in general insurance companies, but we have had an experience where someone fraudulently claimed for the death of his father who was still alive!... We cancelled the policy immediately!

We have also tried, as much as possible, to be apolitical in our dealings but we believe that the government needs to do more on fostering indigenous businesses initiatives as we see in other countries such as the Black Economic Empowerment Program in South Africa.

Recently, there have been requirements to increase minimum capital for general and life insurance companies. This is easier for larger established companies who have been on the market for much longer. When such requirements come into play, we have to think of raising capital. This was quite a challenge in 2015 when we were only 6 years old, but it is easier now that we have grown. However we think the Regulator still needs to foster competition so that not only the big companies, which incidentally have majority foreign share ownership, are allowed to operate in the Malawi market.

When we were starting, our thinking has been that this trend would not augur well for the country after having been independent for over 58 years. Observers would ask "what is wrong with Malawi" because they would say "after 58 years of independence there is no Malawian owned life insurance company" because this is the exact opposite in our neighboring countries like Zimbabwe, Zambia and South Africa.

I believe that the benefit of fostering home-grown businesses means we are providing employment to the nation and ensures that our profits are re-invested in Malawi and not repatriated outside the country.

So fortunately, the regulator has listened to our observations in the past and has come up with risk based capital requirements that are aligned with the classes of business written by each player in the market, in other words, instead of a one size fits all, the capital requirements were based on the risk profile of each player with room for increasing capital requirements as the risk of the player grew bigger.

Hopes for the future

My hopes for the future are really to achieve more growth and as I have already indicated I am targeting to exceed the K5 billion revenue mark. Ultimately I would want Smile Life to grow like the current insurance giants in Malawi. We would like to increase our investments to not only financial but also physical assets so we can own property like the famous Chayamba Building and others and, hopefully, let this company perpetuate itself. Recently we have also played a positive role in the society for example we managed to make various donations including one to the Malawi University of Science and Technology to be used for motivating and encouraging innovation among lecturers and students and to protect underprivileged learners around Blantyre from Covid-19 with 600 face masks courtesy of Smile Life Insurance Company.

How would I like to be remembered?

Finally, I would describe myself and would like to be remembered as a risk taker, just as my profession of insurance is a profession of risk taking. I took the risk and here we are! We now have Smile Life!

2

Newton Kambala

"The entrepreneur who went from the farm to the boardroom"

Mr. Newton Kambala

Mr. Kambala's story inspires the most rural and local Malawian. Here is a child of man who worked on an estate and had a meagre income.

He is now the Chief Executive Officer and Managing Director of Mkaka Construction Company. His story is one that teaches us that anything is possible and greatness can come from anyone even from the most disadvantaged.

Fast facts

Date of Birth: 14 May 1971, Blantyre Malawi
Company: Mkaka Construction Company
Industry: Construction, Civil Engineering
Countries: Malawi, Zambia, Zimbabwe
Achievements:

- Past Chairperson for the National Construction Industry Council.
- Past Council member and an Executive member of the Malawi Institute of Engineers.
- He has served on boards of several companies in and outside Malawi.

Past employment

- World Vision International
- ESCOM (as a Counterpart Engineer to Lahmeyer International GmbH on the Tedzani III Hydroelectric Power Scheme) and
- The Malawi Polytechnic (As a lecturer).

Education

- Robert Blake Secondary School, MSCE, 1983
- University of Malawi The Malawi Polytechnic: Bachelor of Science (Engineering), 1988

Humble beginnings

I am Newton David Kambala, I come from Lilongwe from an area called Nambuma, My father lived a nomadic life because of the type of work he was doing. He worked in a private farming company owned by the late Mr. Wallace. So he was moved around from farm to farm. The company comprised of several farms including Chikhwawa estate in Salima, which was the first farm he worked on, Mbavi estate in Lilongwe, Khasu, Mudi, Kasonjola, Makoka and a few other farms.

I went to school in the farms and lived a typical village live. My father did not have a senior rank and was doing very low grade jobs. This meant that our family background is a very low income background.

The foundation, getting secondary and tertiary education

There are 10 of us in our family and I am the 3rd born child. Though the first and second born did not do well in school and as a third born I gave some hope to my parents since I was the only one who managed to go to university straight from secondary school. I had my secondary school education at Robert Blake Secondary School from 1979 to 1983.

My ambition was to become an engineer although I did not know what being an engineer entailed. As a young village boy I thought engineering was all about repairing equipment such as maize mills and cars etc. that's all I knew about engineering until I came to the University of Malawi at the polytechnic. I was disappointed when I started my studies because I thought what they were teaching us was not engineering and a couple of us started to argue with our Professors saying "we came to do engineering but what we are doing is not engineering".

So our lecturers had to explain that what we think is engineering is not engineering it is actually more relevant to being technicians and mechanics and that engineering is actually about designing and creating things and as such it requires learning a lot of theory and involves a lot of calculations which is what we were learning.

This helped us understand the purpose and relevance of the course we were doing. In those days there was only a single 6 year engineering degree that started with a 3 year diploma and proceeded for another 3 years for a Bachelor of Science in Engineering. It was not specialized apart from the final year in which you were asked to choose and major in one of three disciplines between, civil, mechanical and electrical.

I naturally wanted to major in mechanical engineering, since I was a born mechanical engineer. I understood mechanics a lot and loved it the most. However the choice of a major was being made in the second year of the program. I choice mechanical engineering but fortunately or unfortunately my Lecturer, Dr. Ben, advised that "everyone can tell that you are a born mechanical engineer from the way you pass your exams and your assignments. You would therefore benefit to diversify into another specialization such as civil engineering in order to complement your nature". I did not like this advice, but fortunately or unfortunately my young brother, Justin was in the same class as me, who also chose mechanical engineering and Dr. Ben advised me that "since both of you are from the same family you would benefit a lot from doing different things and Newton can as well do civil engineering since he understands mechanical a lot" After so much contemplation and inner struggle I eventually came to a point where I at least considered his advice. Finally, I found the strength to accept his advice and decided to major in Civil engineering.

When I look back today, with hindsight of course, I see that that was a very good decision to make because I don't think that I would have achieved what I would have done in my business venture or as much as I have achieved, had I chosen to major in mechanical engineering.

My working life

I qualified with a Bachelor of Science in Engineering in 1989 and immediately found a job with World Vision International. I worked with them for 1 ½ years and decided to quit because I was both the first and only engineer for the company. This meant that everything I did was new and well received by the organization without much criticism. Everything I did was very impressive and people were praising me for every little thing I did. However I knew that for me to develop as a professional, I needed to be among other professionals who would criticize me, teach me and polish my skills. I therefore knew that this was a wrong place for me. I therefore decided to leave and joined the then "Electricity Supply Corporation of Malawi" (ESCOM). The motivation for me to leave was purely because I wanted to get some practical experience. My hope was to get relevant experience with the hope of running my own business in the future. So I joined ESCOM in December 1990 and worked there for 5 years.

During those 5 years I gained a wealth of experience and had a very rare opportunity to be involved in a very large project for the construction of the Tedzani III powwer station which is very rare for most engineers, considering the nature and scale of our current projects in Malawi. This was a huge project and involved tunneling through a mountain for about 1 ½ kilometers. And I was responsible for quality control and approval of onsite designs. Apart from the current Valé railway project there are probably few projects that would compare to the scale of the projects I was involved in. I was working a minimum of 15 hours a day and mostly 18 hours a day with onsite practical experience.

After the project I was privileged to be attached to a German engineer, Lamar international in Frankfurt. It's an 18th Century business and very well established. The head office I was attached to was roughly two towers of 50 floors each mostly occupied by engineers, amongst the few administrators and accountants etc. It was a company where people who had worked for 20 years or more would not know each other unless they were working together on a similar project. I was also privileged to learn about other fields of engineering such as firefighting engineers, chemical engineers, aeronautical engineers and many other fields within engineering.

On my return to Malawi I was a very valuable employee and managed to finalize the Kapichira III project. I was then asked to relocate to Kapichira but due to family priorities I failed to relocate since at that time I wanted to ensure that my 5 year old son's education is not disturbed. As a result, I decided to change jobs and eventually found employment with the University of Malawi, the Polytechnic where I became a lecturer from January 1996. I taught as a full lecturer which is unusual because universities do not allow you to become a full lecturer with only a bachelor's degree.

The interview panel was torn between my experience and my perceived lack of appropriate qualifications for the role. I was therefore told by the interview panel that I did not qualify to teach as a full lecturer at the university although they felt that I was the right candidate for the job based on my relevant experience. They therefore wanted to offer me a position of only associate lecturer on the understanding that that is the appropriate qualification for the role and also because it is the only way that the university could employ me and allow me to be considered for a scholarship program for further studies.

I answered that I "look I am too old to be called assistant anything and if you feel that I am not qualified you can leave me out because I am not desperate". However, I was still given the full lecturer role. I was probably one of the best lecturers of my time due to the rarity of my industrial experience, since it was common for lecturers to only teach on the basis of higher education but without any practical experience. It was also common for students to abandon a lecturer's class if he delays for 5 to 10 minutes, but my class would wait for me for more than 30 minutes because they were really keen to hear and learn from my practical industrial experience. I taught for 4 years and during this time I started my business in 1993.

When I look back at why and how I started doing business I think it was just personal passion because by that time I had little understanding of entrepreneurship, I believe that everyone person has the capability to become an entrepreneur but for him to exploit that nature there should be a reason to do so. In my case I think it's because I was coming from a low income family of 10 children and had siblings that looked up to me whom I thought had great potential. It was therefore difficult for me to feel comfortable about my own achievements and benefit alone as an individual without doing anything for my siblings.

Getting into business

I therefore decided to supplement my income and do business for this reason. Looking at the great sacrifices that, in particular, my father made, such as saving for our education for all my then educated siblings and walking bare foot due to failure to buy shoes. I told my father that I will take on the responsibility to pay school fees for my younger siblings. I said this simply because I saw that the sacrifices he was making were too great and that I definitely needed to do something.

Even though I was compelled to help in this way I knew that this responsibility was too huge for my salary alone and that I needed some supplemental income. In an attempt to supplement my income I ended up starting a small household business in 1990 by leaving K20 (Twenty kwacha) everyday with my houseboy. I told him that "after you clean the house go to the market, buy fish from the market and sell it, we will see how much you can make at the end of the day". On my return from work, I would find that he has sold it for K40 (Forty Kwacha) or more and I will give him another K20 for the next day with similar instructions.

I was slowly building up capital while at the same time using the money to assist my brothers and sisters and ensured that I am not tempted to use and spend it on myself. Once I had retained enough I started a business that supplied quarry stones and sand to construction sites. I actually did not have a very large lump sum because I had quite a number of responsibilities. The way I eventually started in the quarry stone and sand supply business was through a little ingenuity. I approached some ladies who were selling sand but had no market. I saw this as an opportunity to make money and I asked the ladies to give me the sand and quarry stone on credit. Because I was new to them they all refused to sell me the sand and quarry stone. However I managed to convince a single lady to sell me on credit. I was given stones at K40 per bucket and I paid her from my proceeds later. She was so excited with this that she started telling her friends and very soon I had a ready supply of quarry stones.

I ensured that if I sold the stones for a higher price I passed on some of the higher profits to the quarry stone ladies. The ladies were very motivated and increased their production. They grew confidence in me and trusted that I would not steal from them. Because of that my business started rolling much faster leading to higher proceeds. I was however experiencing problems with cheque payments since I had no formal business name or business bank account. I then decided to register a small business called Neba and partners. "Ne" was for Newton and "Ba" was for my wife. Later on I managed to buy a car at K4,000 to facilitate my mobility. It was a very old thing, not really in one piece, and perhaps better described as "pieces of moving iron sheets". I bought it from the taxi rank and when driving it I could literally see the ground below me. Just like "Fred Flintsone's" car. It was very old but it did its job and made my business a little bit easier.

In 1991 I met a friend and former class mate of mine, David Mzandu, who asked to join my business. I told him that the business is too small and I think I need to do it with my wife. If we are to do business we should do something bigger and more organised. So we decided to do some construction business and registered a construction business with him and Mike Kachere, who later worked for the commonwealth in England as a finance person with a Bachelor of Commerce degree. He is a cousin of mine but we brought him in, in order to balance the skill. We thought that 2 engineers need a finance person to properly run the business.

We then decided to come up with a name together, and in true Malawian fashion we played around with or names and then came up with the name "Mkaka construction". The letter M is for "Mzandu" "Ka" for "Kambala and "Ka" for "Kachere".

The first registration was Mkaka civil contractors but at the time of registration it was registered as a sole trader because Mike had then pulled out and David Mzandu was now working for the government and therefore this was a conflict of interest. After 2 years, David was quickly promoted and he had to resign due to the growing conflict of interest.

I then started doing business as a sole trader with a focus on civil works. We were operating from our house as the company's office and the only full time employee was my young brother and some temporary workers. We had no machinery and were only using the normal picks and shovels. After 3 or so years we started buying some smaller pick-up vehicles then we progressed to buying slightly larger 3 ton vehicles and then 10 ton lorries. That's when we started catching people's attention that there is a business here. We later moved our office from our house to an office in Blantyre. We rented a small room at the corner of Rajani enterprises near the Blantyre round about or the then "Kandodo corner shop" near Malawi Post office.

In the year 2000 we decided to incorporate the business and rename it Mkaka Civil Construction Company Limited from Mkaka Civil Contractors.

I was the principle shareholder with 85% with my brother and contracts manager with 7.5% each. Within my shareholding there was also my wife's shareholding through the shareholding of Neba and partners in Mkaka Construction Company Limited. I appointed a board of directors with the chairman as Mr. Ken Mthunzi. He is a very able chairman because he controls me a lot and I have given him all the required powers, he is actually my boss and I have told him that I do not need him if he cannot control me.

Looking at how I started business, I believe that had I been comfortable in a job I would not have started business.

Hurdles along the way

Looking at how the fortunes of the business over the years I feel we had quite number of challenges from the very beginning. As all businesses we did not have enough working capital and it was not easy to convince any bank to lend us some money. I then borrowed K1.1m which helped us to do business better when we bought some trucks in 1997. It's only after we bought these trucks that the banks started calling us to enquire if we needed any funding.

We started to experience growth of at least 15% annually however in 1999 to 2001 our growth dropped a little bit because of where I come from. The then Government thought that because I was from Lilongwe I was loyal to the opposition party and the government of the day said "we cannot give you any business".

This was the beginning of a very difficult phase because it was a very lean period since the government said they will penalise anyone doing business with us and hiring our equipment. At the time we were the only local company that had bought a grader and a small excavator using a loan of K6.5 million from Indefund. The fact that we had a huge loan for machinery that could not generate any income for us was a big burden for the company. I was the first indigenous Malawian to buy a grader. But fortunately, business started to pick up again in 2002 when the government finally started giving us work again. The reason for this turnaround was not intentional by the government or at all voluntary.

In fact, the European Union started questioning the government as why the company is not getting any work when in their view the company was a very promising contractor and also because the government was supposedly advocating for building the capacity of local contractors. So overtime when there was a government meeting with the EU they were always asked why Mkaka construction is not given any work. The government could no longer hide their intentions and gave up on their ban on us. They were therefore compelled to resume giving us business which contributed to our stabilisation.

We had specifically large problems in 2011 and 2012 due to the shortage of foreign exchange leading to the government's failure to procure and maintain a steady supply of fuel in the country. During this time we had just bought equipment but could not use it because there was no fuel in the country. This was a difficult time for the company because we had borrowed K500 million from the bank for our capital investment into equipment and the failure to generate revenue was particularly difficult.

In this time our turnover dropped from about K993 million to under K250 million and after the audit we confirmed that we made a loss of K250 million in 2012 and profit of K298 million in 2013. After the change of government in 2013, due to the untimely death of the late Dr. Bingu, Wa Mutharika, there was an improvement in the fuel situation though the foreign exchange shortage took a little more time to overcome. As a result in 2012 we made a profit and eventually sustained these profits.

Critical success factors

We are one of the few indigenous companies with proper governance structures and we try to employ professionals in all critical positions. We have both a good management team and strong team of directors. I also put a lot of value on the audit process, and give a lot of value on the report on internal controls. We always strive to resolve issues that are raised by the external auditors and Continue to implement further audit and directors' recommendations in our audits.

Currently our business is expanding across the Malawi borders, into Zambia and Zimbabwe. We also continuously setting revenue targets for the business.

3

Rachel Sibande

Malawi's Technology Super woman"

Dr. Rachel Sibande

Rachel Chimwemwe Sibande is a Malawian technology expert, computer scientist, STEM educator, and entrepreneur.

Sibande founded and directs Malawi's first technology hub called "mHub". It nurtures young technology enthusiasts with technical and entrepreneurship skills. Its software development unit empowers young Malawians to champion the development of local technology and provide local solutions.

She has championed development and deployment of innovative technology solutions in agriculture, public health, elections monitoring, citizen engagement, disaster management and digital financial services in more than 14 countries.

Rachel Serves as Program Director, Data Development at the Digital Impact Alliance, within the United Nations Foundation.

Fast facts

Date of Birth: 9 January 1986, Lilongwe Malawi
    Company: mHub Limited
    Logo:

Countries: Malawi, Africa and beyond, wherever duty calls.

Achievements:

- She was named as one of the 100 most Influential African Women of the year in 2020.
- In 2019 she was a recipient of the "Forbes Woman Africa Gen Y Award" at the Forbes Africa Summit, South Africa

- She was recognized as a "New Wealth Creator, by Forbes Woman Africa" in South Africa.
- In 2018 Rachel won the Climate Smart track to innovate and invent award at the Next Einstein Forum (NEF) Global Gathering in Rwanda for creating a thermal chemical process that generates light for microgrids.
- In 2017 she won the award for "Young Visionary Leader of the World at the World Youth Forum
- In 2012, Rachel became an alumna of President Obama's Young African Leaders Initiative
- Named by Forbes Magazine as one Africa's 30 most promising entrepreneurs under the age of 30 in 2016
- Listed as one of the top 40 innovators under 40 in Africa (2016)
- In 2016, Rachel became Malawi's Ambassador of the Next Einstein Forum Initiative which promotes science, technology engineering and mathematics (STEM)
- Sibande delivered a Technology Entertainment and Design talk in 2013 on the subject of using technology for agricultural development.
- In 2016, she became the first local licensee for TEDx Lilongwe
- She has provided technology solutions to general elections in the region in Malawi, Tanzania, Zambia and Zimbabwe.

Education

- Our Lady of Wisdom, MSCE
- University of Malawi: Bachelor of Science (Computer Science), 2006
- Mzuzu University: Master of Science in Information Theory, Coding and Cryptography, 2010 (with Distinction and an average of 80%)
- Rhodes University: PhD Computer Science

Rachels story

I am Rachel Sibande. My Father Ben Chavula is an accountant by profession and my mother, Ethel was a teacher who taught Home Economics and later pursued and qualified in rural development work. I am the first born in a family of six and I have 2 sisters and 3 brothers. I have a brother, Ben, who is a medical doctor, the other brother Blessings is an economist working in the banking sector. I also have a brother Dave, who is a professional in the hospitality and tourism industry. My other sister is a stay at home mom and another sister, Faith who studied for a business degree.

I am married to Chrispin Sibande and have 3 children. My husband is a human rights lawyer. Our first child is a girl named Uwemi meaning "the goodness of God", the second is a boy called Uzengi meaning "the one tie the binds us together", and the third is a boy called Unenesyo meaning "God is righteous". They are all Tumbuka names.

As I grew up, my parents expected a lot from me and no expectations were lowered just because I was a girl. A typical lesson of performance not being gendered. This helped to push me forward in life as I was expected to do well in everything, there was no laxity or statements like "its ok you've failed in math because you are girl" no not all. I grew up with a strong passion for languages especially French and initially aspired to be a French translator or anything related to the French language.

However, when I was 12, I noticed that sciences are more challenging and I was curious and wanted to know how phenomenal technologies like telephones, radio transmission and television worked. To satisfy my curiosity, I decided to study sciences and particularly computers. I proceeded to study a Bachelor of Science at Chancellor College with a major in Computers and minored in statistics. Statistics was for the love of mathematics since this was a passion of mine and computers for the curiosity of how things work.

My postgraduate was a master's degree in cryptography which is the science of coding and decoding messages to ensure there are secure systems. And well, you can only secure a system if you know how to ethically break into systems. I have also obtained a PhD in computer science from Rhodes University in South Africa; again it was out of curiosity. I have always been curious about science and mathematics because from youth I wanted to discover new things, and the world of science helps you discover so much about our world.

In my career, I started off as a programmer who was developing accounting systems with Globe Internet at a time we were supporting Sage and were developing an Enterprise Resource Planning Package meant for the Sri Lankan Market and the rest of the world. This required me to understand accounting concepts, so I had to enroll for a diploma in accounting. I proceeded to teach at Kamuzu Academy where I taught Information Communications Technology and Mathematics, and then to Mzuzu University, where I taught Statistics for 2 years. I then joined USAID funded projects in agriculture as a market information system specialist. The project was called the Market linkages Initiative. It was in 7 countries including Malawi and it involved use of a web to SMS market information system to enable farmers access market information such as crop prices, and agricultural farming advice. I then became Deputy country Director and later Country Director. Through this experience I gained a lot of knowledge of project and people management which has proved invaluable in everything else I do.

So, in 2014, I embarked on developing citizen engagement technology initiatives for elections monitoring. Together with an American business partner; we built a platform for citizens to verify voter ID through mobile without having to queue. We also developed a platform for independent civil society observers and citizens to send real time reports on incidences as they happened during the election. We have deployed these platforms in Malawi, Mozambique, Tanzania and Zambia. We are currently working on developing a "community of practice" of individuals from the region that can have the capacity to deploy such technology solutions in their countries during elections.

In 2012, I was privileged to participate in the Young African Leaders Initiative program; and there I was exposed to a hub, an entrepreneurship hub for all types of businesses. I liked the idea and thought of replicating it back home in Malawi and of tailoring it to my interests by ensuring that it caters for technology, innovation and then entrepreneurship. I then started reading about hubs which was a new concept across the globe with the Kenyan ihub being among the maiden hubs in Africa.

I learnt from research that most hubs had not been sustainable partly because the business model was based on membership fees of upcoming entrepreneurs and income from desk space or co-working space which is insignificant to the related costs as a whole. So I wanted to start something that is sustainable and not to repeat what had failed and perpetuate the cycle of failure. I therefore went to learn from the Rwandan hub, KLab. I found out that their hub is heavily subsidized by the government in various forms such as free space and part operational costs catered for. It was evident that the Rwandan Hub is very progressive and dynamic in various ways. I also studied the Zambian Hub; Bongo Hive and adopted them as a mentor hub that we could learn from.

After, learning from the various existing hub models; I developed a business model for mHub. I decided that apart from providing support to entrepreneurs through the traditional services like digital skills and entrepreneurial training and provision of a co- working space; as a hub we would also establish a commercial entity that would generate profits from developing commercial technology solutions. *I realized that the biggest capital and asset I had was my intellectual capability to build technology solutions*.

The mechanics of setting up mHub were that I was closing off one of my projects at USAID and planning to pursue my PhD. However I thought to myself "there is no way I would thrive if all I am doing is nothing but my Phd" so I decided to keep myself busy with something I am passionate about and that will feed my curiosity.

So as MHub we build technology solutions and we build websites, mobile applications, systems, data collection tools whether web, mobile, SMS, USSD you name it and that is our core stream as a business.

So, our model is a business, which develops technology solutions and ploughs back profits for social good. As a social entity; we train children, girls and youth with digital and entrepreneurial skills. We run the children's coding club, a girls coding club and a Robotics club among other initiatives. We also run the Lilongwe Pitch Night platform to mentor and expose emerging entrepreneurs to the general public and potential investors for enhancing access to finance, markets and skills development.

The majority of our clientele are either international organizations in Malawi or organizations outside the country. For example, we have provided platforms for technology platforms in Mozambique Zambia, Tanzania, Angola, Zimbabwe, DRC and Angola. We are currently expanding and now have a Zambian office and we hope to extend to the rest of the continent as we hope to extend and grow.

I would describe myself as an assertive, determined and tenacious individual who really wants to see what I envision come true. I believe in people and that has helped me with mHub because at first the people I worked with, including my parents and spouse did not fully understand the concept of what I wanted to do but along the way they caught on and we made progress. The good thing is that they supported me even if they did not fully understand the concept.

The name mHub ought to have been "Malawi" Hub, but since Malawi is a protected word, I thought "M" would do just fine. What we do at mHub is to nurture young innovators and entrepreneurs. We created a working space that sparks creativity in young innovators. For example, we have a "Wall of dreams" where innovators write their dreams of what they would like to achieve in life. We have a lot of artwork that sparks a creative mind and we have tried to use locally available resources to create something beautiful from them instead of discarding them and damaging the environment.

Our working space accommodates all sorts of innovators in various fields. They simply walk in and tell us what they do and what innovation they have. We then provide mentoring and coaching and networking.

We also run the national entrepreneurship challenge in which we search for great business ideas that will create great social impact and reward the winner with $30,000 as a way of overcoming the challenge of access to finance. One of the winners we have had has been working in food processing of tomatoes into tomato paste for example, and there are many other entrepreneurs we have helped.

One of the challenges we have faced is that of forging partnerships. We have seen that this takes time and requires a lot of patience. So, my advice to young entrepreneurs is that things take time but if you have vision and are focused and you consider some strategic partnerships somehow, they will mature. And, your greatest capital is your intellect and knowledge.

This leads me to my favorite quote that "start where you are and start with what you have" because there is never going to be a time when all conditions are suitable time. I think people fail to start because they are waiting for their million-dollar capital and everything to be set but life doesn't turn out like that. People procrastinate a lot and this leads to people dying with their ideas and enriching the grave where such ideas are useless.

As the hub grew, we won an award from the Next Einstein forum which is an initiative that seeks to find the next Einstein from Africa. The innovation that won us the award was my and my partners project to solve energy challenges in Malawi. These challenges include lack of adequate and stable electricity. Our idea was to use maize cobs to generate combustible gas that can power a turbine to generate steam and energy. The financial prize we got was reinvested into the hub to help us buy biogas equipment from South Africa.

The other project I find useful and that was done as part of my PhD research is a local web based application in which citizens can submit reports on their perception of service delivery, on various services including water, electricity, sanitation and waste collection. So all the service providers are using this technology to track citizen reports in real time.

I was also honored with an award at the world youth forum and was recognized as one of the 13 visionary leaders of the world. I received the award in Egypt and was also asked to speak even though it was a surprise.

One of my mentors from Google gave me a book called "dealing with the imposter syndrome". The book said whenever you are in self-doubt you need to look back at the things you have achieved and ask yourself 'is it normal for me to then start doubting myself.' " And I believe you are your own greatest asset, in spite of failures and at times lost business. I have always encouraged myself and self-encouragement has been critical to my continued success.

This is also what helped me to overcome the fear of starting the hub. I think believing in yourself is very important because you will often find yourself in situations which no one but you believes in yourself. The art of self-affirmation is therefore very important, and this is some-thing we need to learn. I like what Muhammad Ali said that "impossible is nothing" because impossible is just a word people use to scare you.

I affirmed myself against most stereo types of gender, stature and so on and in fact I have used these biases as my fuel to deliver and prove them wrong.

Another project we have is the use of basic SMS to report human rights violations including sexual abuse. There will then be various support and interventions that are done to support the victims. We are also developing the energy concept in an earth energy company.

Along the way, I made some self-assessment on things I need to improve on. One was my writing skills, and I needed to write and communicate well. I need to step out of my reserved comfort zone and decided that when I go to a new place, I should at least speak to at least 3 people that I have never met. I needed to communicate well and sell myself, so I developed my 3 second pitch, my one minute pitch and

I saw great improvements. I needed to think fast on my feet so that even if I meet someone from the rest of the globe, I would be able to stimulate a conversation.

I also embarked on reading books and outside my tech zone, so I had to invest in soft skills and leadership books as someone who manages, deals and leads people. I have read books by Robert Greene, and other books like "people mastery", "48 laws of power" and I realized that I was using some things in the books without me even knowing about it. Currently I am reading a lot about Rwanda. I realized that reading outside your comfort zone makes you a whole person and I realized that at the global level their definition of a smart person is one who can engage others even in unfamiliar conversations. Otherwise outside that I just want to be alone and be myself and be with my family.

But I see young entrepreneurs who say they don't like the publicity and personally and if I had a choice I would not want to see all the information about me that is on the internet right now and for you to believe it, I am not on Facebook, but those are the sacrifices you have to make. You have to transcend the challenges of not being a public person.

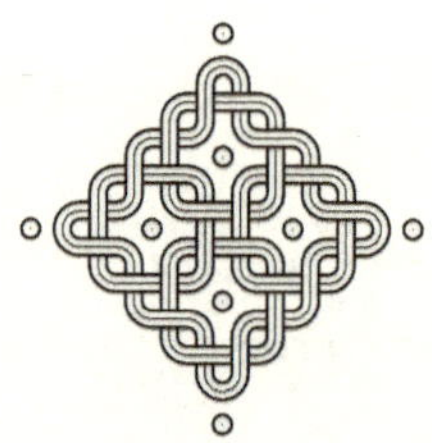

4

Mark Katsonga

"The entrepreneur who constantly reinvented himself"

Mr. Mark Katsonga is the Group Chief Executive officer of AGMA Holdings. His journey has been long, interesting and not free of pain and disappointment.

He is an entrepreneur who has mastered the art of constantly re-inventing himself.

From fruit selling to tailoring, candle and polish making, to virtually being manhandled out of his own cosmetics business, Candlex Limited Malawi, he is one who used his reinvention skills to still make a name for himself in the market place!

Against all odds he ventured into poultry and the public bus business and made it big. He continues to re-invent himself with other group ventures and he is surely an entrepreneur to learn from!

Fast facts

Place of Birth   Nneno, Malawi

Company   **AGMA Holdings**
Comprising

- Axa Coach Service
- AGMA Estates
- AGMA Motor Centre.
- AGMA Trust

Countries   Malawi

Education

Atlantic International University USA, Mater of Business Administration
University of Zimbabwe: Advanced Diploma in Marketing

Mark's story

My name is Mark Katsonga, born in the then Blantyre District that was later subdivided into Blantyre and Mwanza and then Mwanza was further subdivided into Mwanza and Nneno and I was born in the current Nneno district. But when I was born it was simply one Blantyre District.

I grew up in a village called Nicholas Village in a traditional authority Mlauli. I did my primary education in Nneno while my secondary education was only partly in Nneno, partly in Blantyre and partly in Harare Zimbabwe which was called Salisbury at the time. I continued with my College education in Marketing from Zimbabwe and Currently I hold a Masters in Business Administration from Atlantic International University from the USA. Other short courses have been obtained from Holland at Helsinki School of Economics and Finland at Maastricht University.

My business interest started way back when I was in primary school where I started selling things such as mandazi and zitumbuwa. I would also buy things from other parts of Salisbury, and sell it at school and I continued this until my secondary school days.

My police service saga

I got my first job in 1971 in the civil service specifically in the Police Service where I worked for 4 years. Interestingly I ran away from the Police Service and went back home to my beloved mother, I actually I walked to my village in Neno and late in the night.

I argued with relatives at my home village who wanted me to go back to the police force and only listened when my mother told me to go back immediately and not waste a good opportunity like that. I then walked back to the police training school, and though I had initially lost interest for it, I turned out to be the best student of the 30 past squads!

I was naturally tempted to do business again and this, after all is said and done, landed me out of my job. I would buy the fruits that are abundant in my home district such as oranges and tangerines and sell them in Blantyre. However the government was very strict at the time and did not allow civil servants to do business and unfortunately my fruit selling business was somehow discovered.

I bought some potatoes on credit but could not find a buyer until they went bad. The seller eventually pitched up at my office to complain. I was called to the office and to my surprise, found the seller there. The moment I laid eyes on them I knew things had gone south for me. I explained myself and we resolved the matter with the seller that in fact I had not stolen from them but actually failed to sell the produce.

I went through a disciplinary process and lost the promotion I ought to have received though the reasons were not relevant to business and after being frustrated I moved on and left the civil service. I joined Southern Bottlers in mid-1975 up to the year end. My business interest still developed and I thought I needed to invest in a proper education since I had not obtained a college education by the time.

My Zimbabwe adventures

Since I was not excited by the course content in the Malawi colleges I chose to go to a college in Zimbabwe. It was a difficult decision to make but I knew that I had a gap in my business knowledge and that I would not be able to graduate my business from the selling of oranges, tangerines and potatoes to really big businesses in the corporate world if I remained as such.

This realization dawned on me after moving from the civil service to the private sector at Southern bottlers. Since previously the business I was doing was really a side business and more of a past time, I discovered that at Southern Bottlers, unlike the civil service, big business is "serious business" and I knew that with my secondary school education I could not easily make it and succeed in the corporate world.

Though I had some interest to pursue an education while I was in the civil service, I was unable to afford it due to the low pay, but I was able to have some savings at Southern Bottlers and ultimately managed to send myself back to school in Zimbabwe. I opted for Zimbabwe due to its proximity and relative affordability compared with other international universities in the USA and UK. So I paid K39 for my air ticket to Zimbabwe and I was there for over 2 years after which I came back home with a qualification in Marketing.

I was now more valuable and had several job offers since my qualification was rather unique in the market. I attended interviews at Press Corporation, Chipiku Import and Export, and Lever brothers. I was interested in Lever Brothers since they had the most attractive package at the time and I joined them in october 1977 as an area sales manager and management trainee which was the common format of jobs at the time.

My tailoring adventure

I enjoyed the job at Lever Brothers with its good salary and benefits, however, the passion to do business awakened inside me and I was at pains at deciding what business I would do. I then decided that I would go into clothing and tailoring. I did some research on how to do the business and felt that I had enough knowledge of the business and I set up shop in 1980. However, being a novice and with hindsight now, I discovered that I had big knowledge gaps.

I bought machinery from Taiwan, found a nice building in Ndirande Goliyo, and setup a factory. I partnered with a friend who studied tailoring in the UK and there we were doing business again. The challenge I discovered was that this industry was already dominated by Malawians of Indian origin. We thought an easier niche at the time was going into uniforms since we did not have market connections or shops for selling normal clothes like shirts and trousers and so on.

But it was not easy to do business because of an already saturated market, limited capital and the lack of practical knowledge in tailoring because I had more knowledge in homecare products based on my work experience. I later discovered that I was doing a more steady business and seriously considered resigning. However it was so tough because this was no longer a side business but it was the "only business" and I had to survive on it and yet it was failing.

Soon a friend of mine who was working at Old Mutual offered me a job as a sales representative. I was forced to accept the offer though it was a low level position. Fortunately, I was not married at the time and I was "suffering alone" as a bachelor living with a friend and sharing a house. I still felt uncomfortable to work but had little choice.

So in 1982 I decided to sell off the business because I thought I needed to concentrate on my new job. I then approached one Mr. Likungwe the owner of a rapid steam laundry. He was not interested in the business but referred me to his brother who was retiring and perhaps would be interested to invest his earnings in this business. His brother also declined the offer and decided to retire in Zimbabwe. However Mr. Likungwe then suggested that "why don't you just put the business in the paper?" I thought it was a good idea but I could only afford a small advert, and yet this yielded ten applications and what I noticed was that only 2 of them were from Malawians and the rest were from non indigenous Malawians. I told my auditors, Graham Carr, about my intentions and they said let us review your applications. There was a Mr. Mervil who wrote all the interested people and told them the minimum price is such and such. The bidders started competing by biddind for the business until the final bid was K25,786. This man kept pushing his bid by K786, and there were two things I did not know.

Firstly that this is basically a miracle number because the Arabic phrase *"b-ismi-llahi r-rahimi" which means "In the name of God, the most gracious, the most merciful"* not only precedes every chapter of the Quoran but is represented by the number 786 when the letters are added up using the Abjad numerals. Therefore the use of the number 786 is extremely popular in the South Asian world. *(The abjad numerals are a decimal numeral system in which the 28 letters of the Arabic alphabet are assigned numeral values. They have been used in the Arabic Speaking world since before the eighth century when Arabic numerals were adopted. In the modern Arabic, the word abjadiyah means "alphabet" in general).*

Secondly I did not know that Indians were no longer allowed to go into small scale business. This was the policy of the late Kamuzu Banda because he said that if a foreign investor comes to Malawi he must invest in more capital intensive industries for which Malawians may not have the immediate or sufficient capital. That's why we see the serious investments of southern bottlers and Illovo Sugar for example making capital intensive investments in Malawi but these guys wanted the business because they could not get a license and they said if we get the business and get the license we can then expand the business. So the sales price of K25,000 was not small money and just to give perspective, my first job as a police officer paid me K18 per month and my second job at Southern Bottlers paid K56 with a sales commission. My management job at Lever brothers paid me K350 and at the time I was starting business the Kwacha was stronger than the dollar, at a rate of $1.31 to K1. So this was no small money indeed.

However out of all the applicants received one man stood out but all them said we are only interested in the business as long as we also get to buy the license. But I discovered that actually I was trading without a business license and I needed to get it in order to sell the business. And that's when I discovered that Indians were not allowed to do small scale businesses in Malawi.

The total assets of my company were K6,000 with debts of about K12,000 so the buyer said I am paying this for the license because it was an insolvent business. So I went to the ministry of Trade and requested a license in addition to the letter of permit to do business. The junior staff said this was an uphill battle, but there was a passionate man who thought there was a good economic cause in the application for the license. His name was Mr. Mkolesya. He handled this for a while and we made several trips to Lilongwe but as we pursued the application the man died. This was a set back because there were not many who were interested in assisting us. Then came along another gentleman who said, though my friend has passed, I can continue to assist you. This man referred the matter to the Undersecretary who then proved to be very busy which made the application to be too difficult to process. I was advised by a Mr. Makako to reach out to the Principal Secretary (PS), but it was a difficult thing to do because PS's were very dignified people not only in those days, but even today.

After some thought I decided to gather some courage and call the PS. I called the PS and explained the hiccup I was experiencing. He confirmed he had not yet received the application but he committed to assist since in his words, "it was a simple matter". I could not believe what I heard, here I was shivering before the PS, on the phone! and then thanked him for his assistance. I told Mr. Makako that the PS will assist me, he took it to the very same Undersecretary with the instruction that "Bwana needs the file now". The Undersecretary then took it to the PS and the following day I got a call from Mr. Makako that the license is done.

I could not believe the speed at which things had happened. I told my buyer about it and he said "are you sure?.... can we go to Lilongwe now?" but it was already about midday and if we were to travel to Lilongwe it we would arrive after working hours but he insisted that we still go and sleep over. I convinced him to travel the next day and true to his excitement, the man knocked on my door at 4 am in the morning! I was still sleeping! No kidding! so we started off at 5 am. We arrived at the ministry who advised they had issued a license to me and then we cancelled it and issued it to Mr. Patel. Mr. Patel was shivering in disbelieve and joy.

In fact we had been using his car several times as we followed up the license from the very beginning of the matter. So on this particular day, his excitement was immense and fortunately I managed to talk him out of travelling on that day also.

We went straight to Graham Carr because they were keeping the money in trust until the deal was finalized. Mr. Patel paid his balance on top of his initial deposit of K12,500. Graham Car then paid off all creditors of about K12,000 , excluded my working capital of about K4,000 or so and remained with K18,000. So I put K15,000 into a fixed deposit account with National Bank and kept K3,000 into my current account to see what I could do with the remaining funds and "reward myself" after all my hard work on the license.

My candle making business

I still worked for Old mutual but I took time to do some introspection and think about what really caused me to fail in my previous business. So I looked at my strengths and weaknesses. What struck me most was the very simplistic market research I did for the business because I did not really know the ins and outs and the real challenges of the business. Essentially, I chose the business because I thought it would be simple to do.

So I decided to still do business but with proper market research. I embarked on my own research and went into shops and studied the various products that were there. I looked at where it was made, what were the requirements and ingredients and so on. I had to use business directories because there was no internet at the time. I went to the chamber of commerce and embassies because I wanted to know who the suppliers of various products were. I did this for about a year and then ended up choosing 1 product, candles, this product was simple to make, not commonly manufactured in Malawi and with only one company producing it only as a sideline product of its main cosmetics business. It was so simple to make that it only required two raw materials, one of the raw materials, was wax, which I would import with the other raw material, wick, being locally available from David Whitehead and Sons.

At that time, exchange controls had just started because of the global oil price crash which prompted many controls to more closely control their foreign currency reserves. But we had to apply for foreign currency to buy machinery at $4,500 which was about K3,900 due to the strong exchange rate and I paid duty of about 6%.

I then poached staff from the cosmetics company, Ramona

Cosmetics, by sending a relation to talk to some of their disgruntled customers. I told him to meet their workers when knocking off and ask them if they are happy. I found 2 disgruntled employees who were not happy with their pay and their poor working conditions associated with Indian businesses. They confirmed that they know how to make candles and I took them on board because we had no knowledge of the candle making business. I also took my house servant as well and the 4 of us started a candle making business somewhere in Chirimba.

However, I discovered that I had still made a mistake on the candle making machine as I did not read the specification very carefully and it so happened that the machine could only make candles of a very small size. I simply decided that I had no choice but to continue. But a miracle happened because due to the exchange controls, most importers no longer imported simple things like candles. And the market was completely dry of candles.

The bright side was that the very small candles were cheaper and did not need a lot of raw materials. In fact the initial sales price was 10t. When I was selling the candles, every wholesaler and all shops said please bring all the candles you can make. There was so much demand for my candles and the orders were so overwhelming. In fact the turnover was so high that by the time the bank facilities and line of credit I had set up for the machinery had matured, I had turned over my stock so many times to the extent that I did not even use my fixed deposit investment. The machine paid for itself. However there was one problem.......

The house I was operating from in Chirimba was so dilapidated and I had to repair it. The land lord then discovered that I was literally minting gold and he became greedy and started increasing my rent. I was charged a rent of K40 per month when I started, but three months into my lease he increased it to K60. I tried to reason with him without any success, and in the sixth month he came again asking for K100. I decided that this was unfortunate but had to find new premises. I could not even think of going to town because it was very expensive so I only had to go for outside town or other cheaper areas.

I identified a place along Chikwawa road at Green Corner. The building was also dilapidated but I thought it could be fixed. I enquired whom it belonged to and the owner was happy to let it out. It had been idle for many years and he said I would have to fix it and that the costs would be set off from my rent. However, I experienced the same problem of increasing rents. We then disagreed on what amount would be credited to my rent and he soon pushed up his rent from K150 to K250 per month.

I was fed up and decided to buy land from the government and went to the ministry of Lands. I was assisted by an officer who told me of land in Chirimba. I said "this is too far from town" and he advised that there is land in Maselema but all the good land is taken, the remaining plot is close to a river and very swampy. There was another applicant who took application forms but had not returned his forms. In fact may people saw the land but had not been interested because it was very swampy. There was a small dry piece and if my factory was not too big perhaps it would fit, he said. I was also told that the application will be treated on first come first serve basis and that if this applicant submits his forms before me he would take the land.

I filled the forms the very same night and submitted them in the morning. Within a month I was given an offer and started constructing. There was no structure in the area and it was all bush! I put up the structure up to roof level but I started running out of money. The reason was that it was now difficult to import raw materials due to exchange controls leading to unprocessed forex applications and no forex. So though my candles were still in demand I had no raw materials. I then took an initiative to get a facility to import a bigger machine. So while the machine was in transit I ran out of money. I explained to IndeFund who were not impressed, and were, frankly, angry that I had "made a mistake" of not planning my affairs properly. I wanted a further facility to finish of the factory I was building and they refused to finance me. So I went to my commercial bankers, National Bank and met a Mr. Everret. He studied the financing agreement I had with Indefund and highlighted a clause that said that whatever I own and will own in the future belong to Indefund until the loans are repaid. He advised that because of this clause he would not be able to give me a facility.

On this discovery We went to Indefund with Mr. Everret and the first remarks were

"why are you here? Do you know what this man has done? He has done things without telling us and now he has burnt his fingers".

But Mr. Everret said

"that's why I am here, because I have been dealing with new entrepreneurs and they make these mistakes but I see success in this man so I want to assist him. This man is my customer who owes me K20,000 in overdraft and he owes you K150,000. National Bank can write off K20,000 without even feeling it but my knowledge tells me that K150,000 is so significant to Indefund and I want us to look at his agreement. Your agreement is unfair to him because you are securing your loan on all his assets both personal and business investments and I can't give him money. Please exclude his house from the security and let the security be his business interests alone such as land and machinery and let both national bank and Indefund rank paripassu (equally) in the security after we finance him".

He further said

"I had a similar case with a young entrepreneur in Mauritius whom we financed but made the same mistake as this man has done. I stepped in to assist him and as I speak this man is the biggest paint manufacturer in Mauritius and is even exporting and I am willing to invest in this man".

He insisted that he goes to the board. I was then told to prepare a cash flow projection, which I did by hand, correcting it with tippex and so on. I got the help of a Mr. Chokani Mhango who helped me prepare a projection seeking K150,000 which was later approved.

Because my problem was foreign currency shortage, Mr. Everett instructed Indefund that they both write to the Reserve Bank of Malawi that even though forex was scarce, they should assist the little business men whose requirements are less than the those of large corporates. And that these small entrepreneurs are the future of the nation. I was also assisted by a friend who said I know the head of forex at Reserve Bank and he accompanied us on a trip to Lilongwe to see the Head of Forex who was then shocked that this was the case.

We were told to go to our bank and it would be approved. All my applications amounting to K150,000 were approved. Shortly, my overdraft was raised to K150,000 from a meagre K20,000. Business resumed, I finished the building and the new candle making machine was installed. Now, I had both the small candle and the large candle machine and I made a lot of money and stabilized in business and this made my name.

later, I went into related products and I started producing floor, polish, soap and beauty products. I became a case study for Lever brothers who were being hit hard and they could not understand how a local Malawian could become serious competition. In fact, at the time we had grown to 400 employees.

I had a colleague called Mr. Katola who offered to sell me his building that is just next to my factory here at Maselema He came to me and said he is selling his property which was a building at a price of K1.3million. I offered K800,000 and he refused on account of having another buyer from south Africa. He later came back after the South African buyers failed to buy his property. I wanted to pay him but he insisted on a lawyer and involved a lawyer who received a deposit of K450,000. But the next time I saw him he came complaining that the lawyer had spent his money and is nowhere to be seen. Because Mr. Katola had an urgent need for school fees we enlisted the help of his banker Fincom who agreed to receive my payments on his behalf.

Since I had a new building, I started looking for a rice processing machine which I found in Indonesia. I decided to build an office com-plex and I contracted Circle Plumbing at a price of K800,000. However Multiparty politics then came and the Kwacha was floated at K4:$1 and within a space of 6 months the rate was K45:$1. This affected a lot of importers including me. At that time I was owing $600,000 to my raw material supplier which was a mere K2.4 million and manageable con-sidering my monthly turnover of over K1 million and annual turnover of about K15 million. However the floatation of the kwacha made the debt to grow to K27 million against a turnover of K15 million per annum. This was bad and the business was so shaken that my supplier got very worried.

I went to all the banks in Malawi who declined to assist due to the uncertainty that came with the new multiparty democracy and its new economic policy. So the supplier who knew exactly what they were doing, said lets buy 50% of the business and we will loan money to the company for procurement of materials. I accepted because the only options I had were to declare the company bankrupt or save it through some type of arrangement. So they did this and business operations resumed. When they saw the high profitability of the business they starting squeezing my shares through the need for fresh investment, and they did this repeatedly and they were converting this into shares until I became a minority in my own company. I was devastated considering all my efforts and the investments I had made, and how far I had come.

Reinventing myself

As a business man I decided not to be put into a corner. I remembered that I had a poultry business which I had started earlier before. This was a small business with 100 egg laying chickens. So I thought I could commercialize it and indeed I expanded it. I also resorted to utilizing a farm I had bought some time back in 1987 in Mwanza called Agma Estate which I bought when Agricultural Development and Marketing Corporation (ADMARC) was divesting I decided to use this farm for my poultry business and it started well. I invested in the business through new equipment and use of a Japanese aid grant and I also set up operations and structures in Mapanga so that I was at one time the biggest egg producer in Malawi. This was the same time I became a minority shareholder in Candlex but the relationship with my Candlex shareholders continued to sour and though I was a board member, I decided to resign from the board.

I decided what to do next and embarked on a trip to Holland to buy additional equipment for my poultry business and in their show-room there was a bus. On further enquiry I was advised that they also sell buses.

Out of goodwill I encouraged them to sell buses in Malawi because the state owned Bus Company was struggling. However, they challenged me to run a bus company but I thought it's too big a business for me. But they offered to assist me if I was interested in running this business. This sparked an interest in me and on my return I started researching the business and studied an existing company called Shire Bus Lines.

I discovered that it failed due to simple mismanagement. I prepared financing proposals which I submitted to the banks and National bank was the first to respond. They financed three buses for me. After I started operations they exited the market due to the frustrations the market was experiencing from Shire Bus Lines, they had numerous breakdowns, changes of schedules, and a lot of cancellations which just made their service rather chaotic. So once I started operations I literally took the market by storm.

I added two more buses but Standard Bank later approached me to respond to my initial financing proposal. They financed 22 buses. Shortly after this National Bank also came along and offered further finance for a further 18 buses! As a result I had fleet of 40 buses in Malawi.

Incidentally I did not buy my buses from the supplier in Holland due to the outcome of my own research on pricing and logistics and so on. However all the other businesses I have done are still there and are flourishing. My tailoring business is with Mr. Patel and he greatly expanded it. My poultry business is also still there and is doing well also. I had another small business before joining Lever brothers called International trade contacts which led to the birth of Wool shop. When I was a civil servant I ran Zakumunda supplies and it was bought by Manica to service the refugees and they grew it so big that it was supplying refugees from all most all the camps in Malawi.

I believe that I started with a certain degree of luck, except for the tailoring. I say this I experienced success in all my subsequent businesses.

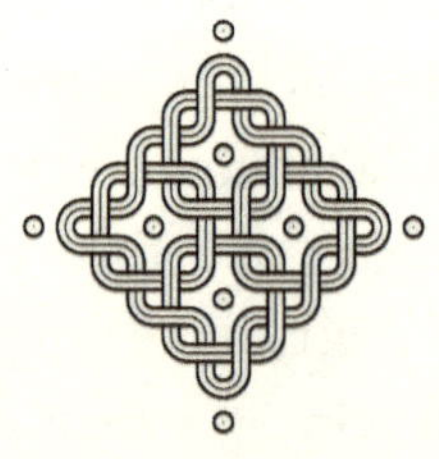

5

Mike Mlombwa

"From Beggar to Billionaire"

The entrepreneur who literally came "from rags to riches"

Mr. Mike Mulombwa

Mr. Mike Mlombwa is the Chief Executive officer of Countrywide Car Hire. A company that offers vehicle hire services.

Mike's story is one of outstanding events. He rose from the depths of abject poverty as a homeless street kid living under bridges and eating discarded food and banana skins, to working as a domestic servant in exchange for school fees to get an education.

Starting with stationery supplies, he later decided to take on the fallow ground of a domestic vehicle hire company. He eventually broke through and is now the single largest indigenous car hire company in Malawi.

Mike is now a billionaire from these very humble beginnings and his is a real life "from rags to riches" story... so... be inspired!

Fast facts

Year of birth:	1969
Place of Birth:	Nneno, Malawi
Company:	Countrywide Car hire.
Industry:	Transportation, tourism and hospitality
Countries:	Malawi

His story

I had an interesting childhood that was significantly impacted by the environment I grew up in. I grew up in my home village in Mwanza mostly with my mom. This is mainly because I was not born in a formal marriage setup since my parents were not formally married and had a short term casual relationship.

I was born in 1964 to this couple and since I grew up with my mom I did not take on my father's surname but used that of my grandfather who was called "Chinyathi". I used this name throughout my early school life until I was old enough to realize that something was amiss with my surname. It dawned on me that I was using my grandfather's name and not that of my father. I then took the courage to ask my mom about my father, about who he was and his whereabouts. I gave her all the questions that come with the feelings of raw and painful abandonment of a child. The main question was "why is he not with us?"

After quizzing my mom, she succumbed to my curiosity and relentless questioning and told me that my father was, in actual fact Mr. Mlombwa. She explained the background of the type of marriage they had, and that my father was not even in the country.

Having understood my parentage; I remained with the ever glaring challenge of getting an education without financial and fatherly support. I had a strong ambition of getting a regular education, regardless of my circumstances, and I knew that I had to make ends meet somehow. So I became creative and practical and decided to earn money in various ways.

One of my first experiences arose out of the village culture whereby even your neighbors are considered to be your relatives. So I was taken in by a nearby family that used to pay my school fees and in return I would do odd jobs like cleaning house, herding cattle, tending the garden and so on. I was also promised that the if I work hard enough the family would continue paying my school fees until secondary school.

However this arrangement was short-lived and did not workout due to their own financial limitations.

I soon found myself helpless again and had to figure out another way of supporting my education. I decided to stay with my relatives who were Adventists and naturally started praying at their church because culturally you ought to pray together with your guardians. So even though my parents and relatives in Mwanza were Anglican I became an Adventist. By and by, I managed to reach standard 8 of primary school but it slowly dawned on me that my school fees challenge would continue. At this stage, my "relatives" who were supporting me were in town and did not continue to do so despite promises that I would be supported through secondary school as already explained. I therefore had no choice but to return to the village to be with my mom, grandfather and sisters. I stayed in the village for several years and became quite hopeless.

At this stage, feelings of abandonment by my father were even stronger and I secretly resented him for my predicament. I still thought, however, that I need to locate him and perhaps get his assistance. I therefore quizzed my mom even more and she gave in again to my persistence and told me told me that my father was from Mahuka village in Mulanje and that he stayed in Lirangwe in the district of Blantyre where he remarried and had children.

He later fled to Zambia due to his being a Jehovah's Witness who in those days were not very well understood by the government of the day, mainly on account of not fulfilling their "feudal duties" of paying taxes. Consumed by the desire to know my roots, I decided to go to Lirangwe. I travelled unbeknownst to my mother, and in the middle of the night, all the way to Lirangwe which was more than 60km away. I managed to locate the Lirangwe village of my father and introduced myself.

They welcomed me heartily and told me that I really resemble my father and the relatives I had found there, I found some sisters and an elder brother Mr. Noel Mlombwa. They said "your father is in Zambia, he also got married there and has never come back, we only hear about him just because some business people who go to Zambia told us that he is still alive. They took me to a place called Mchere to the homes of my fathers sisters and brothers but they were also helpless and could not assist me in any way. I also managed to locate my fathers younger brother who used to work at the Malawi Housing Corporation, and was staying in the Blantyre location of Ndirande. I approached him and shared my passion to finish education and the challenges of school fees. He graciously started to pay school fees for me and not only me but also for my other brother at Ndirande primary school. But, barely a year later, he told us that "I had a dream in which I was told that I should not keep you in my home". This was a shocker, who does that? and why use a dream as an excuse? why not just be forthright and say I can no longer keep you in my home?

After this I went back to my village and later proceeded to Mangochi where I was staying with a brother. He was a brother because as indicated before that according to our culture in the villages you can call each other brother because someone is simply a neighbor. I stayed there for almost 2 years and I was schooling at Mpondasi primary school. I was promised that I will go to distance education centres for my secondary school but it did not work out, also due to their own financial constraints.

Striving in the village

At this stage, I had tried everything and was feeling very frustrated. I decided to go back to the village where my mother asked me more about my trip. I explained my sorry adventure to her saying that "Mom I have tried very hard to get an education and to work and raise money, I have tried everything! But things are not working out as I thought they would, the people who promised me an education just abused me and used me as their servant, so I have decided to come back home and think what I should do next." However my mother, bless her soul, welcomed me with a loving and generous heart and with open arms without any condemnation or taunting at all.

Shortly afterwards, the village headman gave me a piece of land for me to work on and the village elders together with my mother started looking for a good woman for me to marry. In those days in the village we still had arranged marriages. It so happened that even though I was given an option to live a customary village life, whereby I would have had achieved the key village milestones, of marriage and farming, I remained unsettled and unfulfilled in my mind. I felt that something was missing, there was a constant drive in me to do more and push on because I constantly admired my friends who had finished secondary school and some had even gone to university. I always wondered, in dreary self pity,

"why me?"

"why can't I achieve what others have achieved?"

"why can't I help my mother who has sacrificed a lot for my life? Just as others do to their parents?"

I resigned to my fate, painfully so, and settled into village life and started burning charcoal for sale along the Matope road from Blantyre to Lilongwe, now called the M1 main road. Matope means "muddy" and it was called such because it was dusty road and in the rainy season the rains would make it muddy.

Today as you drive this road will still see this age old charcoal trade being plied on the Mwanza road all the way to Blantyre. Some will start off in the wee hours of the morning with 4 or 5 bags of charcoal worth no more than $8 or $10, that's how far I have come, from selling charcoal by the roadside to where I am today.

However, while in the village each and every day I was remained troubled and I constantly asked myself

"Is this the end of my life?"

"Is this how my life will end?

"Or maybe I should try again?

"Just once more perhaps?

"Perhaps so that this should be the last time I try?"

Venturing into the concrete jungle

Then, one day, struggling with my mediocrity and challenges, and consumed by my passion to achieve a better life, I simply took off in the dead of night to Blantyre. I took off at 10 pm on foot. Knowing that I am leaving my wife to the care of my mom and customary village life I had so successfully and very easily achieved. Now, my mom would not know where I was going and even I did not know where I was going!

In those days it was relatively safe to walk alone at night without fearing meeting any thugs and robbers who could ambush you. I walked the distance of more than 83km and arrived in the early hours of the morning the very next day.

This was in 1985 and at that time the plan I had was the only plan I could ever had thought of, and this was mainly to earn a living though working for people since I did not have any relative in Blantyre. I decided on moving from church to church so that the pastors can find me someone who can pay my school fees in exchange for a job in their home or anywhere. However, I was straight from the village and homeless in a city I was not accustomed to and was definitely not an easy sell. I was not convincing, no one knew me and I was just dirt poor! No one trusted me enough to give me what I was asking for, not even with the help of pastors.

I would sleep in the streets with guards of shops of Indian merchants. I told the guards my story and where I had been trying to look for piece work and they accepted me in their company. I went all over Blantyre, in locations like, Chilomoni, Chirimba, Soche and Limbe and in all these places I was told that

"you can try us again later, we currently don't have any jobs for you". Now, on my 6th day, I went to a large church in Ndirande called the Ndirande Seventh Day Adventist Church where I met Pastor Tsoka who was the resident pastor of the Church, He is now deceased, God rest his soul. I told him my story and it so happened that he was also from the same district of Mwanza. I even knew some of his sons and he took a liking for me and was willing to help me. He told me that

"there is a businessman who may need my help. His name is Mr.

Ackim he is a very well-known businessman, I will try to talk to him" and he soon arranged for me to meet Mr. Ackim.

When the day came to meet Mr. Ackim, it was around 6 pm and he quizzed me meticulously. He asked more about me with a great level of caution in case I was dishonest and had ill intentions of stealing from him. He later decided to give me a chance and said he will "try me out". He told me to "go back and come tomorrow".

And true to my routine I went back to the streets in the company of the guards in order to sleep in their safety. Because I was helpless and had no money, I used to live the life of a homeless person. I would bathe in the Mudi River under the bridge, where I would quickly wash myself very early early in the morning before the streets would be littered with the traffic of people walking to work.

I used to eat leftovers from dust bins or from the streets. Banana peels and leftovers were a common delicacy for me, since when people throw away bananas, they would still be edible for at least two to three days. I soon learnt that a banana left over would sometimes have the base that would be abandoned or banana sellers would have some poor quality bananas that would still make for a worthy meal. So that's how I survived.

But on this particular, day, this "Mr. Ackim" day, I was thrilled to have been given the opportunity once again to get an education and earn a living. I was happy that I was leaving the life of a homeless person for the last time, and would live it for just one more night. On the day I was told to report for duty, I took what would be my last bath in the river and set off to my new home.

Mr. Ackim took me into his home on the arrangement that he would pay my school fees and I would run his errands at home and I stayed with him for approximately 4 years. I would wake up everyday at 3 am start cleaning the house and then would wash his 6 personal vehicles in the morning. By 6 am he would find a clean house, ready breakfast and everything else in the home of 7 children.

He was, at the time, trading in the diesel business and asked me to become his cashier and run business errands to buy things for his business. He was very impressed and pleased with me because I was trustworthy. I would give him an honest report of all expenses and remaining funds. In the course of time, our relationship grew stronger to the point that we were relating just like relatives would relate and people thought perhaps he was my uncle. He would give me a little allowance with which I would support my mom. She would periodically come to town but not to the house or place of work. She normally sent a message from a distance and I would go out to meet her and ask how she and everyone else is doing especially my wife.

However, over time his reliance on me was so much that he was relying on me in almost everything to do with his business. Sooner rather than later, some of his relatives were envious of his trust in me and, as surely as the sun rises, stories started circulating that I was stealing money from him, and he later became suspicious of me and became unhappy.

When I finished my education I had a simple pass and obtained my Malawi School Certificate of Education ("MSCE" which is an "O level" equivalent). But I had no result that would give me chances for a college education. On reflection I realised that I barely had had time to study in view of my 3 am house chores and later the business errands. I had to make peace with my predicament and started thinking of what to do next. After getting my MSCE Mr. Ackim now told me that our mutual objectives had been met, he had helped get me an education and besides he was getting pressure from his relatives about me and he now had to let me go not only from his home but also from his business.

His words were like a sharp dagger piercing deep into my heart and I was very downcast. I pondered through all this deeply and tried to look at the situation critically. I knew I had to be strong and deal with it like a man. So firstly, I appreciated that I had at least had achieved something that I had been striving for without much success for a very long time and that is a secondary school education. I picked myself up and decided to "be a man" and "make a plan".

We then parted ways and I started staying in Chilomoni. By then I had a girlfriend who is now the mother of my two lovely daughters.

Chimwemwe and Chikondi Mlombwa. My girlfriend was coming from a very well to do family and we started our relationship when I was staying with the Ackim family. She actually thought I was his relative and had no clue that I was actually a servant. She only discovered this when I moved out of his home. She was working at Blantyre print as a sales representative and we stayed together in Chilomoni in a humble one bedroomed house.

The only thing I had to my name at this point was a radio that I had managed to buy with some little savings made when staying with the Ackim family. I had hit another low point in my life and was overcome with feelings of confusion and self-pity. I would think of my relatives in my village, my mom and sisters and wallowed in self pity and depression. I then asked and constantly thought to myself "what should I do now with life?"

The beginning of business ventures

It did not take me long to act on my resolve to "be a man" and to turn to the only asset I had to my name, my radio.... I then mustered the strength to sell my radio and I sold it at K450, bought some curios and went to South Africa to sell the curios. In those days travelling was difficult because of the war in Mozambique so in order to be safe we had to travel through Zimbabwe or Zambia to South Africa. But my venture was not easy due to accommodation problems and all the expenses related to business. I would only make a meagre profit, if at all.

My wife's parents used to stay in Zimbabwe and I then had an idea to sell zitenje (traditional women's cloth) and women's plastic shoes called "Sofia" in Zimbabwe which would sell much better, so I thought. I would stay there for a month or two but it later did not pay dividends. I then went back to the curio's business and went to South Africa and managed to make R2000. By mere chance I happened to pass by a stationery company called Rice and Company and an idea came into my mind.... I saw an opportunity in the stationery business that I had not thought of before.

I went in the shop and told them I wanted to buy their product. The available stationery was computer printing paper of which I wanted to buy R18,000 worth. I told them that I only had R2,000 but that I would sell it quickly and come back to repay my balance. Effectively I was asking for a loan from a company that I never new, looking back I don't know what emboldened me to ask for such terms on a first time transaction but I believe its my naivety and culture of honesty I had carried from back home in Malawi. I thought they too would "simply trust that I would not disappoint them". But they said no! And quizzed me on who I was, where I come from, which country and so on and so on.

Fate was on my side and perhaps they were amused at my naïve passion and honesty that they later said they can only do this if someone can guarantee me and assure them that know me. Luckily Mr. Ackim was also living in South Africa at that time and was also selling curios at a much larger scale than me and I approached him to guarantee me.

He agreed to put his reputation on the line and came to meet with the management of Rice and Company and to serve as my guarantor and they allowed me to pay my R2,000 and get the stock of R18,000. After paying my initial deposit I told them to simply send the goods and I would see how to clear them in Malawi, the goods were sent by courier to Malawi and I eventually cleared them. After clearing the goods Mr. Ackim continued to discuss with Rice and Company and to represent me as a guarantor. He later asked me the details of the companies to which I wanted to sell the goods but I felt uncomfortable to respond to this but he persuaded me to reveal my customer because he said he was serving as a "guarantor" and did not want his reputation to be damaged in South Africa.

Upon his unrelenting insistence I told him the name of the company. Later on he hijacked my deal and approached the company. He even wrote the government of Malawi that the custody of and proceeds of the goods should not come to me but to him. Eventually Mr. Ackim just sold the goods and did not remit any funds back to Rice and Company. There was then a tussle between us because I had to be refunded my R2,000 and the total cost price still had to be paid to Rice and

Company. Things had now gotten ugly and the issue went to the fiscal police but the Malawi Government cleared me with Rice and Company but after the dust had settled Mr. Ackim only paid me R1,000.

This was yet another major setback following many others before, but in the same spirit of picking myself up I had to reinvent myself and decided to become a stationery sales representative for my very good friend Mr. Jack Kamwendo, He had an office in Dossani House in Blantyre and I mainly worked on a commission basis and would earn commission of say K100 per day which in my day was very good. In total there were four sales agents but I was the only one who really performed a little better than the rest.

Meanwhile at home, I was facing some marital challenges, mainly because my wife was on a stable job and I was earning very little, so it happened that my wife would have extra marital relations and have many boyfriends. It was clear that because I was not earning much she did not respect our marriage. The only thing I quarreled with my wife was that she had many boyfriends but because I had no money I had no say. Later in the marriage these problems continued to the extent that I divorced her. We went to court where I presented my problems and she admitted that she was really unfaithful. At the time we had two children and the custody of the children was given to me. My wife said to the courts that the children were more attached to their father and I raised them alone from the ages of 3 and 1 year old. But I continued to trust in God through this difficult phase of not only single parenthood but the single parenthood of a father.

With the commission that I was earning, I decided to start my own business. Instead of being an agent, I quit and was then just buying and selling products within Malawi. We would buy our stationery from Asians who were not allowed to sell on a retail scale. So we bought from them in bulk and resold in Malawi. Over time I opened an office in the same building Dossani House alternate to my friend and former boss. We then started operating at the same level with my former boss and still managed to maintain a cordial relationship and could compete for the same business and submit tenders to the government.

The genesis of countrywide

After some time in the business, to be exact In 1997 when I was 28 years old, I bought my first car a Datsun 120Y with the savings from my initial commissions and later my own stationery business.

In those days we used to compete with current Indian stationery giants but we were overtaken in the era of multiparty democracy when they seemed to have stronger connections with the government of the day and were awarded bigger contracts.

I chose not to give up and thought of expanding my small business further and was on the lookout for opportunities that seemed promising. I then moved to Newlands in Chigumula where I stumbled on an offer to buy a piece of land and a house in the Moneymen area which I took advantage of in my search for more opportunities. Since I had always wanted to build a lodge I started developing the property I had bought and built some very small structures in the process of coming up with what I thought would be a fully-fledged lodge in the future, more like in "the sweet by and by" to be honest, especially considering the meagre resources I had.

At this time I was ambitiously registering small businesses, and really small businesses they were, in the name of my children such as Chimwemwe and Chikondi general dealers and later on Mike General dealers after my son from my second marriage. I then decided on changing the name of my businesses to something that was more palatable, and decided on calling it Countrywide group of companies. Looking back at the form and size of these business they were more like castles in the sky than established operations. But its not a crime to dream right? This is a free country!

At the time of registering my businesses and after buying my Datsun, I soon bought a second and then a third car. But I recalled what my mother told me long ago about my father. She said he had a taxi and I thought "perhaps I could go into a similar business" because at the time I had 3 vehicles. Among some of the businesses I registered, I had Country Wide Car Hire, along with Countrywide Construction Company, and other company names.

I eventually started my car hire business after being inspired by my father's business. From 3 vehicles in 1997 I slowly and steadily grew the fleet until in 2005 I had 7 seven vehicles of my own. I persevered until 2007 when I had 10 vehicles (and looking ahead to 2015 they would become 15 vehicles). I started small but later had a breakthrough when I was hired by Celtel to provide 20 vehicles for them. Due to the high demand I had to subcontract and I engaged an Indian to provide additional vehicles. Unfortunately my contract with Celtel was terminated midway and I failed to pay my Indian subcontractor. So he dragged me to court and I discovered that the Indian was playing dirty tricks on me by bribing my own lawyer. So my lawyer was not challenging the case in court until I lost my property in Moneymen. If you go there at a place called Pamodzi lodge you will find a number of complexes which were all built by me and he (the Indian friend) only did finishing touch ups.

My "sweet by and by" dream went up in smoke..... as it said to me "bye bye" it said it ever so sadly, but bye bye it was, and I would not recover that property till this day. Do properties speak you might ask? Yes, I was so attached to it that I could hear it speak to me in sadness. That's how disappointed I was.

I had hit yet another low point in my life whereby after achieving something tangible it was virtually stolen away from me. However, I looked back from where I had come and the path I had taken in life, my humble backgrounds and what I had now achieved andI said to myself once again, "I should not give up and maybe things will still work out".

So I pushed and soldiered on! So much so that I looked at the resources I had at the time, which were 10 second hand vehicles, and I said

"I can do something with these vehicles,

I can do something,

I still have something to work from".

I then approached the banks for financing but they were unwilling to help me. They looked at my profile, educational background and the fact that I did not even have a degree, the type of business that was a sole proprietorship and not a fully fledged company and also that I had no professionals running my business and of course my "lack of extensive experience" in the sector and surely they declined my application.

I still strove and found a second business opportunity during the time when there was a national census in 2008 and submitted a bid to the National Statistical Office who needed vehicles for their census exercise. I fortunately won the contract and resorted to subcontract again by building a network of suppliers across the country. Eventually, I supplied 300 vehicles when mine were only 10 vehicles with the others being supplied on a commission basis of 20%. This was a bold and shrewd move.

From this deal I got paid about K200 million. I deposited the cheque with my bank and at the same time wanted to cash K5 million so that I can celebrate with my mom, sisters and relatives. However the bank denied my application for withdrawal. They told me to come at 9 am and then later at 11 am and this went on until I cashed my cheque late in the afternoon. The bank thought it was a fraudulent transaction and did not expect me, a poor Malawian man to have that much money. Imagine that! being despised by your own banker! That was just sad and unprofessional!

They later felt embarrassed of course when I expressed my disappointment in no few words and after this "minor" incident the banks realized that I was a serious businessman and they started warming up to me afterwards. After this deal I paid off all my subcontractors and bought 20 double cabs to add to my fleet. After wards I was able to approach the banks and get some financing from them, from time to time I don't know what changes they made to their lending criteria, since I had not obtained further education after all.

Though my banking experiences improved, it still was not easy because it wasn't long before I needed a loan to expand further and increase my fleet for a government tender for airport services.... I again approached the banks, but with no luck.

When I approached some local banks for K300 million I was told that I could only be given K35 million and it was only FDH Bank, an indigenous bank that had faith in me and let me borrow K200 million at one go.

Hopes for the future

My vision has always been to establish Country Wide everywhere, and to increase our current fleet to more than 200 vehicles so that country wide is truly "across the country". Today I am able to say that the the company is growing, getting a lot of business from non-profit organisations and foreign embassies, and our driver service is proving popular with international aid agencies who use Countrywide and so we are steadily expanding our fleet.

We have a lot of customers and therefore can't satisfy everyone. This means we continue to sub-hire from other rental vehicle companies to meet the demand. As we continued to grow we opened a branch in Lilongwe in 2014 and another branch in Mzuzu in 2015 including branches at Chileka and Kamuzu international airports.

I would also like to expand to other countries and I am busy looking for good partnerships. As for my current businesses I am also bringing in a lot of professionals to manage my business interests which is very important for continuity.

Because business is ever changing and competitors always enter markets, I am thinking of diversification so I don't put all my eggs in one basket. So in 2018 in addition to our own earnings, we sourced financing and started building three five-star hotels in the commercial capital Blantyre and Chintheche on the shores of Lake Malawi with a total capacity of 120 beds. We aimed to offer packaged deals of car rental and accommodation for these new locations. Its an achievement that gives me great pleasure because it is a fulfilment of my long lost Moneymen hospitality investment.

Even though we had a fleet of 80 in 2016 and that was ever growing the Covid-19 pandemic hit our hospitality industry hard and we saw the demand nose dive so much so that we had to drastically cut our fleet and will also be looking for funding to gradually expand as the demand slowly increases. We are a little shy to borrow locally considering the very high interest rates in Malawi and we might be considering foreign borrowing if we deem it more affordable".

My hopes for the future are still to expand my business, and I am currently engaging consultants to provide professional advice on how to expand. I am looking for suitable partnerships to expand the car rental business to include trucks, specifically to cater for regional freight and I also aspire to take Countrywide Car Hire cross-border.

One day, if you travel to South Africa or Kenya, there will be a new contender, a new name for car rental – Countrywide. Once that is achieved, I will say I have accomplished my mission.

But we operate the business in a very competitive environment which international players with a lot of financial muscle. Sometimes the competition is such that they want to price you out of the market by undercutting. However Malawians are now slowly, ever so slowly, coming together to help each other in business. They are now realizing that it's better to help each other as Malawians because helping non indigenous investors is usually temporary and short-lived.

I am now the president of the Indigenous Business Association of Malawi, my role has taken me to several countries and I admire how these countries protect the business interests of its people. In South Africa and Kenya there is black economic empowerment, Zimbabwe and Zambia all have indigenization offices. In Malawi its becoming difficult because of the current economic power of the foreign busi-ness men that have been entrenched for a long period of time and it requires strong resolve to change this and start empowering indigenous businessmen, but we are currently working on such policies. I think we can't achieve it alone without concerted effort and government support. But I started this organization for this very purpose, because I wanted to encourage indigenous businesses in Malawi.

Final thoughts

I am grateful for where I am in life because considering how far I have come. I can't believe what I have achieved and that God has given me a name in this world. I am now able to educate my children when I myself struggled and struggled pathetically.

I am therefore passionate about educating my kids, because I know what it means to struggle for a good education. I struggled to get an education but I decided that this is not a struggle my children will have. So I invested in their education and sent them to the best schools I can afford. That's my priority, so my two girls went to Monash, and the others to Saint Andrews International High School and Kamuzu Academy.

I am still in touch with the family of Mr. Ackim who is now deceased and when I meet his children we are just like brothers and sisters, and everyone else who helped me in my life I make it a point to recognize and appreciate them very well.

I also go to the village and chat with my relatives and on one occasion I met the woman my parents gave me for a wife. When I asked her who I was she could not recognize me until I reminded her who I was and we continue to chat. She now has 10 children... she remarried of course!

In the year 2000 I lost my mom to cancer after a longer battle and a lot of attempts to save her life. Her death meant that I had now lost both my parents after my father had also died several years back.

I would however like to be remembered as a man who cares for and cherishes his family.

I always encourage young business men not to rush in business, to seek God's guidance and to reinvest their earnings in their business. To do things at the right time and tell them it's not good for them to live a lavish lifestyle too soon.

When I am asked to tell my story I always use the topic "From Beggar to Billionaire". Why I say beggar is that there are two types of a beggars. Others beg to consume and squander their earnings but I was a beggar for a purpose. Sometimes when I look back I cannot believe the achievements that have been made in my life and think I am dreaming.

I ask my self
"am I still alive or not?" or
"Am I in heaven?"

I have to pinch myself and comeback to reality because my background was so difficult and yet I am now well known both within and out of Malawi. Sometimes when my international customers are introduced to me they cannot believe the simple person they see. They don't even expect a Malawian to own such a successful business. Another thing I noticed in Malawi is that Malawians don't work together to pool capital and do something big they all do it individually which is unlike other cultures that propel themselves into business through partnerships and combined efforts.

I hope to be remembered as a person who left a legacy, as someone who faced and overcame unsurmountable odds, and never gave up!

6

Dr. Thom Mpinganjira

"The innovative and unrelenting financial engineer"

Dr. Thomson Frank Mpinganjira

Dr. Thomson Mpinganjira is the Founder of FDH Financial Holdings Limited.

He is a son of Malawi who has truly built a business empire that we should all be proud of.

He has served as CEO of Stockbrokers Malawi, Malawi stock Exchange, First Discount House and FDH Bank and of course FDH

Financial Holdings. His experience ranges from stockbroking, share trading on the stock exchange and discounting of financial assets.

He goes down in the history of Malawi as a pioneer of innovative financial services and products in Malawi and who dared to go **where angels fear to tread.** He bought the Malawi Savings Bank which he later merged into FDH Bank.

Against all odds he is the entrepreneur **who did not and could not give up!**

His story is laden with the tenets of unrelenting resilience that lies beyond his charming exterior.

Fast facts

Date of Birth   28 February 1961, Blantyre Malawi

Company   FDH Financial Holdings

(Comprising FDH Bank, Malawi Savings Bank (Now part of FDH Bank), FDH Discount House and FDH Money Bureau.

Countries   Malawi

Financial Information

Total income : K44bn,

post tax profits: K14bn

Total assets: K235bn

Information is for the year ended 31 December 2020

Education Zomba Catholic Secondary School, MSCE, 1979

University of Malawi - Diploma in Business Studies, 1982

University of Malawi - Bachelor of Commerce (Accountancy), 1984

Association of Chartered Certified Accountants (ACCA)

• Fellow Chartered Accountant

- PhD in Entrepreneurship, May 2015

His story

My name is Dr. Thomson Mpinganjira, born in Blantyre on 28 February 1961. I was born in a family of eight of 4 boys and 4 girls. I have mostly grown up in Blantyre. My primary school education was at Kanjedza and Misesa primary schools and later at Zomba secondary in 1979. I later went to the University of Malawi from 1979 to 1984 where I got a Diploma in business studies in 1982 and graduated with a Bachelor of Commerce Accountancy in 1984.

I worked with Deloitte from 11 June 1984 to 1989 and later Blantyre Printing and Publishing as a Senior Corporate Accountant. I moved to Mandala Motors in 1992 until October 1994, and progressed to National Bank in November 1994 as Head of Risk and Security and on 1 September 1997. I joined Stock Brokers Malawi as Deputy CEO and later became CEO on 8 January 1998 at a time when stockbrokers Malawi and the Malawi stock Exchange were one entity whereby the stockbroker was used as an exchange in keeping with the model of emerging stock exchanges in Africa. I served as CEO until 31 march 2000 when I went to setup what is now the Malawi Stock Exchange and was at the Stock Exchange from 1 April 2000 until 31 May 2002 after which I joined First Discount house (FDH) in the FDH Group.

Financial services in those days especially stocks and stock broking were a new phenomenon in Malawi but it all started with my employer Deloitte, who head hunted me first to join Mandala and later Stockbrokers in order to replace an expatriate who's contract was shortly coming to an end. Plus, at the time, I felt that growth opportunities were limited at National Bank and this allowed me to easily move. The environment at Stockbrokers was totally new in many aspects with much better perks. There was also a lot of technical training and travel around the region such that I was sent to the Zimbabwe and Botswana stock exchanges for short periods of about 3 to 4 weeks on each visit, at a time when the Botswana Stock Exchange was just starting up.

This is really what led me to do the banking business, that is, the exposure to the financial services industry through stock brokers in shares and investments in treasury bills which were the main instruments at the time. I also benefited from the contacts and the knowledge I had regarding shares and treasury bills since even banks did not venture into this business and I was the first Malawian to venture into it.

In the period of 1997 to 1999 I got the opportunity to connect with some people from whom I got the idea of getting into business. I established my contacts through my regional travel in the Southern Africa Development Corporation countries and international travel. During these travels I went to the International Finance Corporation (IFC) who sponsored me to go the Securities and Exchange Commission in Washington DC, and later trained in private placement of shares in London and South Africa. These regional and international partners would prove very handy because when setting up I needed a lot of technical partners and investors and these where the very people I reached out to when setting up.

The other thing was that I had a good relationship with my first employer because they were the ones that were head hunting me and placing me in the market. When I look at why this was the case I think we just clicked with the partners and managers particularly John McClean and Sean O'Neil who were partner and manager respectively. Actually I should have stayed on but I left as a Senior Accountant which was a managerial level.

While working with Deloitte, I was assisted in my house hunting and when I found a house, it was in area they did not recommend. They thought it was not suitable for my status as someone who is earmarked for internal growth in the firm. They wanted an area and type of house that would be good enough to entertain clients of any type. So I got my current house and unfortunately it was my undoing in the firm because I got it through a mortgage and soon discovered that I could not afford the mortgage with the salary I was getting. So because we clicked at a technical and professional level, every time a client said we are looking for someone they enquired if I would be interested and since both Mandala and Stockbrokers were their clients, they were able to approach me for opportunities that arose there.

My business and entrepreneurship beginnings

My business career really started when I was chatting with my brother (now Dr.) Peter Mpinganjira who shared me some novel financial services ideas at a time when Malawi only had Continental Discount House (CDH) in this sector.

CDH was led by Ghanaians seconded by the World Bank to the Reserve Bank of Malawi (RBM) on a financial deepening program aimed at restructuring the Malawi financial market so that we have more financial institutions other than banks, and also to bring in new financial products. After the consultancy ended they applied to operate Malawi's first discount house and RBM granted them a license to operate Continental Discount House.

When I heard about this I thought to myself that "even locals can do this business". So I read and researched relevant information and applied for a license from RBM. I approached and invited a team of 5 Malawians to form a consortium and to team up with an anchor institution which was the Malawi Development Corporation (MDC). However one of our partners had to pull out due to conflicts of interest that arose and 2 others also dropped out and only one partner and I were left.

For me to find the anchor partner I first had to hire my brother Dr. Peter Mpinganjira in December 1999 to do a project proposal at a price of K1.5 million, which in those days was a lot of money. In January of 2000 I approached MDC and their board gave approval for them to be the anchor partner and we then registered a company called First Discount House.

Then, on 8 March 2000 we submitted an application to RBM. This process took some time until early 2001 due to subsequent requests from the RBM which seemed to make the process go backwards and forwards and in which I wrote hundreds of letters and attended many meetings.

During this process my remaining partner fell out as well. This meant that I was left all alone but I did not give up. RBM then submitted the application to the Ministry of Finance. In April 2001 the Minister of Finance rejected the license on the grounds that the Government of Malawi is getting out of the financial services industry based on guidance from the IMF and World Bank and that they can't allow FDH to get into financial services. It was a huge set back because I had to start the process all over again and when I look back I really don't know why I didn't give up.

However the governor of the RBM Mr. Elias Ngalande and the then general manager, late Mr. Charles Chuka encouraged me to look for investors in Zimbabwe or South Africa. However at that time I had spent my own money amounting to K4.5 million Kwacha on various things including rentals for 4 offices in MDC house and everything to do with registration and setting up the business. So there was no giving up because I would then have to write off K4.5million so *I did not and could not give up.* And in those days trying to borrow K2.5 million from banks was an extremely huge task even though I demonstrated to them that I had already spent K4.5 million of my own money.

So I approached Press Corporation, who rejected my proposal saying that "we don't go into greenfield and even if we wanted to go there we would want a majority shareholding". I went to Old Mutual Malawi and they practically said "you guys are a joke". So I then went to Old Mutual in Capetown through my dealings with them on the stock markets. During this time I met another general investor Prof. Mfutso Bengo who was interested to get 40% of the business but unfortunately the license application failed. So when I was talking to Old Mutual RSA they were curious why a construction company, owned by Mr. Mfutso Bengo, would be interested in a financial services venture and they realized that there must be potential in the business.

So the very same day I got a response through their representative of Old Mutual investments in Malawi, who was a board member of

National Bank and Press Corporation. He asked for a meeting at the Malawi Stock Exchange which took about 1.5 hours and he advised that Old Mutual was very interested in the deal even though they don't go into greenfield. He also promised to call Press Corporation to consider the deal. So 15 minutes after the meeting I got a call from the CEO of Press Corporation, Dr. Jeff Cowl, asking for a meeting at 7 am the following morning. So I went for the meeting and it was successful in which both Old Mutual and Press Corporation would jointly own 50%. However Old Mutual asked for a technical partner because they don't understand the new line of business and I reached out to my contact in Zimbabwe namely Nigel Chanakira of Kingdom Holdings and Kingdom Stockbrokers. He expressed interest the same afternoon on 11 April . The remaining 50% would be split between Kingdom holdings and myself. However they negotiated my share down to 24.9%.

On 25 July Kingdom Holdings said they would come to Malawi and amazingly enough I got the license on the very next day on 26th July and Kingdom arrived 4 days later. I got the license because I had already presented the technical partners to RBM and by the time Kingdom came to Malawi they wanted more shareholding but could not get it because the license had already been issued and other processes had already began. We started setting up the business by buying furniture software, equipment and similar things. We found office space in Umoyo House where we are till this day.

We also entered into a 3 year management contract with Kingdom Holdings and they brought in two expatriates and their software. I also started head hunting staff for the company and I got Edward Chillima from Continental Discount House and Terrence Nsamala from MDC, a secretary a driver and a messenger and in total we had 7 staff members.

This was done after obtaining approval from my board on September 11 2001 when I was CEO of our stock exchange. The board deliberated on whether I could participate in the investment as a CEO of the exchange or if I should leave the Stock Exchange altogether. They took the whole morning and called to say "you can participate because we don't want to kill the spirit of entrepreneurship, and also because the RBM is keen to have another institute to join CDH. We finished at around 5 pm only to hear that America had been bombed through terrorist attacks on their prestigious twin towers.

During this time I was also facing political pressure because my cousin Brown Mpinganjira had a fallout with the government of the day and was fired from his job as cabinet minister. My family was also targeted with my brother being fired from a government job while my other brother had his business shut down. I knew I was next in line since many politicians considered my business as a front for my cousin's Political party and as a result there was so much mistrust about me.

Our operations started in 2001 when at the same time I was a board member and CEO of the stock exchange. However, in 2002 Kingdom Holdings expressed concern that they are not comfortable to put in money while I am not physically there because they needed someone to oversee operations fulltime. And that's how I ended up resigning from the Malawi Stock Exchange to join the discount house. So I joined FDH as Managing Director on 1 June 2002 after recruiting my successor at the stock exchange, Mr. Symon Msefula.

As business progressed we noted that the market was so dynamic and things were changing all the time hence affecting our profitability as a business. We then decided to diversify by going into banking and stockbroking by following the model that existed in the Kingdom Group. In time we saw an opportunity to buy a local bank when it was under liquidation and management by the RBM. We did a due diligence but did not like what we saw and decided not to pursue it.

There was also an opportunity to buy into Nedbank at a time they wanted to pull out of Malawi. We also did a due diligence and later went to RSA to draft the contracts. However the deal fell through because Nedbank replaced the Regional Director, a white expatriate, who was returning home, with a another expatriate from Zimbabwe. The new expatriate put this sale on hold because there was another sale going on in the group in Mauritius.

Our diversification into banking prompted the RBM to advise that if you are getting into banking you cannot have another bank (through

Press Corporation) as a major shareholder so we had to buyout Press Corporation's shareholding. It was quite a difficult exercise because first we offered a net asset value of K57.5 million which they initially rejected. But later their board accepted to withdraw but said the offer we made is too low and that they wanted K110 million which was almost double our purchase offer. There was not much we could do so we negotiated it down to K100 million and had to find the money between the two remaining shareholders, Kingdom Holdings and myself. But pulled all the stops and we paid them on 4 August 2006. Old mutual decided to stay on at the same shareholding of 20%. and did not want to increase their shareholding.

On 1 January 2007 we set up Stockbrokers Malawi, after successfully paying off Press Corporation and started thinking of what other things we could do in order to diversify our operations.

Along the way, First Discount House needed additional capital due to operational challenges and changes in regulatory requirements. As a result we thought that listing on the Malawi Stock Exchange would be a good way of raising capital from the public. We soon found out that listing a company is an expensive and complex process but once the Malawi Stock Exchange granted preliminary approval we started working like horses driven by patience, perseverance, courage and determination.

We worked on prospectuses and set up a launch date, and invitations were sent out to guests amid a highly charged and excited environment. However a day before the launch I got a letter from the MSE that final approval had not been granted by their board and that the launch could not proceed. Imagine that! We had set up everything for the launch including 3,000 prospectuses and spent over K35m and it all went down the drain! I had to personally call 300 invited guests telling them of the cancel of the launch, I cancelled hotel bookings and all other arrangements that had just been finalized. So this was one of the most frustrating experiences so far.

However, and gladly, we finally got a banking license on 27 November 2007 and Old Mutual and I started setting up the business with our own money. Our head office was in Umoyo house and our bank started with a single branch at the head office in Umoyo House on 15 July 2008. Our next significant milestone of a 5th branch was achieved in February 2009 when we also achieved another milestone of buying a company called "The Money Bureau Limited" on 16 February which we renamed "FDH Money Bureau". The decision was strategic because apart from being in the same line of business it had very ideal locations. They had an outlet at Shoprite in Blantyre, and in Lilongwe they had outlets at Crossroads, City Centre and also NICO center in Old Town near game complex. So the deal provided us with 4 very prime locations in the CBD's of Lilongwe and Blantyre.

Part of our setting up was to persuade our landlord to give us the whole building so as to deliberately remove our competition from part of the building we were occupying. So we ensured that the bank that was in the shared building of Umoyo was moved out and we then set up 3 of our newly acquired 4 locations with a money bureau only at NICO center. You could then say the rest is history!

The acquisition of a bank

An opportunity then came up to buy Malawi Savings bank (MSB). We thought it was an important opportunity because it was becoming very difficult to compete with some of these very large banks in the country. So we went after MSB! Government was convinced to sell MSB because of a Diagnostic Review for the bank, at their request. Generally the report showed that there was a lot of opportunity for improvement as can be seen from public information surrounding bad loans and political influence on the bank. I used this report to inform my strategy on how to address the specific areas for improvement and it proved to be an invaluable resource.

So we bought MSB and the journey was a very interesting one. To begin with so many parties went for the public briefing and so many got the bidding document but funny enough on the day of bid opening, there was only FDH that submitted for MSB and 5 bidders that tendered for Indebank.

Our bidding for MSB was a bold decision. I think if I were not the key player in the bidding process and if someone else was making the decision, it would have been impossible to go after MSB because the risk was just too high as there were risks that were both known and others unknown at the time of bidding. But my motivation was that "look I am a Malawian, born and bred here and if I can't do business here where else will I do business?" So we decided to take the risk and to manage it and handle it once it materializes ....and here we are!

So, funny enough, we got the highest technical score of both bids for both MSB and Indebank. Actually for Indebank we were successful and got the highest technical score amongst all 5 bidders however we ended up being the only bidder for MSB. We also met all the required criteria and the government knew that if we are dropped they may not get another interested bidder because of the very high public interest that would chase away potential investors. Fortunately, our bid was technically and financially sound because all the FDH shareholders were interested in the infrastructure of MSB, and Old mutual was interested for strategic reasons as they would prove handy for their market-penetration strategies in the rural areas.

However, due to a lot of public and political interest surrounding the MSB bid we were forced to add about K1bn to our purchase price. We paid a premium because they thought we would gain from the infrastructure and the customers. However the real customer base was not as was expected when we actually came in because there was and still is a large unbanked population in Malawi at the time.

We hired an accounting firm from South Africa as lead advisors since they worked with Old Mutual in South Africa. They set up an integration management office with specialist teams for various aspects of the bank such as legal, banking, finance and Human Capital consultants among others. This happened from 2016 to early in 2017 and in total we have spent about K20bn on the acquisition, integration, recapitalization and related set-up expenditures.

Speed bumps along the way

However, as with all mergers there are challenges that need to be dealt with such as bad loans, differences in culture and also legal provisions for staff lay-offs. The consultant we employed helped with that but there were also the bad loans that the MSB had amounting to K6bn. Fortunately government gave promissory notes to cushion the loss but the loans are very problematic to collect.

The culture difference remained a challenge because staff were resistant to change since they thought and said "this is the way it has always been done and why should I change?" We did not tolerate that mindset because we cannot have a public sector mindset in a private sector bank and if people can't adapt then they have no place in the bank. We therefore saw a lot of people leaving the bank on their own or because we had to let them go.

The legal risk was also significant, but we managed it by adequately engaging staff. However there were also legal cases at the courts of which we won some and lost some. The real challenge however arose after the retrenchments. Because we lost over 450 people and our numbers in the bank dropped from 1,157 to about 700 people.

The other challenge is that there is a high unbanked population in Malawi and the average Malawian's knowledge about financial products is not very strong. However, we noted that there are ways of getting around this problem by leveraging on technology. FDH has joined the mobile digital revolution which has allowed us to capture a good number of the unbanked for example since launching our mobile application late in 2016 we had seen an additional 60,000 customers to September 2017 and these were active customers with a mobile phone. This customer base is really growing in the urban areas since this platform is a way of sending money to loved ones in the rural areas. This technology has a customer base that is growing more than those on internet banking which is more for office people and corporates. The "FDH wallet" is also an interesting product which allows sending money even to people not banked with FDH, and it can be used for buying airtime, paying utilities and cashing out money at an FDH ATM and so on. So this boosts our fee income and allows for capturing new customers who see a lot of utility in this service.

Another key factor in the banking sector is multi-banking so that customers get various services from various banks. This is common in the corporate banking world whereby they have a main account at one bank and other accounts at other banks for example for purposes of facilitating international forex transactions and so on. The key area of competition for the banks is therefore quality of service which mainly means speed of servicing your customer and also of number of value adding products you bring to the customer. One such product for FDH Bank is called "one click" for payroll payments and other cash transactions with a lot of payments.

Fraud in the financial sector is also a big thing, especially when there is collusion because it is a very difficult thing to beat and most frauds succeed because of collusion and I think it is worse with the digital revolution but the way to counter this is to ensure there are adequate internal controls, and ensure there is segregation of duties, staff holidays and staff rotation.

Illicit financial flows are also another problem that is being faced by the country and this is occurring through aggressive transfer pricing as only one of the many ways in which it happens. The way to address this is to share information with correspondents.

Hopes for the future

Our hopes for the future are that having acquired MSB we can stabilize and growth the bank and its operations so that under the agreement with government we can list on the Malawi stock exchange and offload the government's stake in the bank and also to raise capital for expansion into the region like our colleagues First Capital Bank.

How I describe myself

So finally, how can I describe myself? Well......as a person who, once

I identify something that needs to be done I ensure that it is done whatever it takes and no matter how many obstacles I meet on the way it will still be done!

For example I lost K35m Kwacha trying to list on the stock exchange, when asked to double the price to buy out Press corporation we found a way to raise money and pay them off and also to set up the operations of the bank, with Malawi Savings Bank we still found a way to make it work even after discovering numerous challenges.

Sometimes you can use networking, bargaining and negotiation skills. I have also succeeded through investing in people and in hiring the right skills. My advice is that don't give up!

I would like to be remembered as a trailblazer, a person who inspired others to do things that Malawians have not yet ventured into and someone who made Malawians believe that it is possible to build and leave behind a legacy because my study of Malawian businessmen shows that most businesses die with the owner of the business and I found out ways of making a business sustainable.

To achieve this desire I set up a family trust in 2001 for that very purpose so that it will outlive me and must also outlive the people who run the trust. I was actually inspired by the Indians because the Indians we see today have their roots in the 1800's through to 1908 when they came to build the railway lines. After the railway was done they used their gratuity and earnings to buy land in Limbe and build shops. Their businesses have continued and their children are the ones running the economy now. White people also have a strong succession and inheritance culture so that wealth is properly passed on. So if these can do it, then we can also do it. My drive is not just to set up a business in which you just spend and waste the profits, but for it to live well beyond your lifetime.

7

Napoleon Dzombe

"The multifaceted entrepreneur, my gentle giant "

Napoleon is the founder of Blessings Hospital and owner of Mtalimanja Holdings Limited and has a complex story. He has evolved from being a deliberate secondary school drop-out with raw and almost naïve passion about the wellbeing of his family and community, to a true entrepreneurial giant who has held true to his basic obsession of seeking the well being of others. He is truly multifaceted but purely "community needs" based and philanthropic altogether.

With so many twists and turns until stumbling into his destiny, his story is a marvel to read.

His heart is so warm that he is my "Gentle Giant"

Fast facts

Year of Birth   1958
Company   Mtalimanja Holdings
Countries   Malawi
Achievements

Napoleon has attained the following recognition both locally and globally

1. 2005 Lifetime Achiever Award
2. In 2005 his work was the subject of the 2005 short film, "A Warm Heart".
3. 2006 Community Builder Award
4. 2009 Achiever of the year Capa Award
5. 2012 Achiever of Achievers Award
6. Awarded a PHD in Entrepreneurship *"for an enduring spirit of dedication and inborn desire to use his resources to serve, uplift and empower people including the vulnerable. For his enterprising and generous spirit, for his ability to create jobs; and for being an "entrepreneur with a heart""*
7. Establishment of Mtalimanja Holdings

His achievements has been featured in international media and is a catalyst for mindset change to entrepreneurs both in and outside Malawi.

Who am I?

My name is Napoleon Dzombe. I was born in 1958, I am married and have 6 children. I hail from Nkhanile village in an area called Chakhaza in the Malawian district of Dowa. My father was a businessman who later in life had an opportunity to buy a farm in the district of Madisi. It so happened that due to poverty I later abandoned the farm so that it lay in disrepair and lack of proper management oversight.

The poverty that led to my father abandoning his farm was characterized in other aspects of our family life. This affected our farming activities to the extent that year-in year-out we had a poor harvest and persistent hunger. Every September of the year our family would literally move from one relative's house to another in our quest for food.

How it all began – The motivation

My journey really started when I was in secondary school. I was selected to Dedza Secondary school in 1997 to begin my secondary school education. Throughout my studies I struggled to find school fees in spite of the government scholarship grants. My pocket money always ran out within a month of commencing school. I remember that I would request permission to leave my school and I would buy cassava worth K4 ("K" stands for the Malawian currency called the "Kwacha") and sell it for K8 in order to make ends meet. I would also sell various supplies to my fellow students because I knew I could not call my dad because he too was under a lot of financial pressure.

So, at the end of year 1 of secondary school, I asked my father for a loan of K25 which he so graciously gave me. With this money, I bought flour sieves which I sold during the school holiday. I sold them house to house and made total sales of K125. From this money, I repaid my dad the K25 I borrowed earlier and I paid school fees which was K17 for the first term. The balance, I put in a bank account so that I could pay another K17 and then K16 for the second and 3rd terms respectively.

I developed a curiosity to know how much my teachers earned, and I soon discovered that They earned K115 on a monthly basis. This discouraged me so much that I felt there is no purpose in pursuing education. I then decided in my mind that school was not really worth it. I also wondered how I could take care of my family with the K115 I would potentially earn as a salary one day, if it were a salary comparable to that of the teachers.

I knew I could not feed my family of 11 people with this amount of money. Shortly after this incident there was a school visit by His Excellency the Ngwazi, Dr. Hastings Kamuzu Banda at a farm nearby our school. I was privileged to be chosen to attend this function based on the selection criteria. The criteria was that you must be a high performing student and indeed I was. In a class of 90 students I always attained a single digit grade. Ever since commencing my studies I had never got a grade with 2 digits.

The nearby farm so happened to be that of renowned politician, Honorable John Zenas Ungapake Tembo. The crop I saw there was immaculate and of a marvelous standard. I immediately remembered my father's abandoned farm and mused at what I would do if I were given the opportunity to run it. I wondered at how it would be if the same standard of farming were replicated on my father's farm. Again, I remembered the 11 family members at home and my potential salary. The farm tour was the last straw! I immediately decided to leave school for good and nothing would turn me back now.

I waited till the end of the first term and told my teacher that

"I have stopped school"

"Why" asked the teacher?

"because I want to get rich" ....

My teacher thought I had gone bonkers. My teacher and others, said I was making a big mistake, that I perform well and should succeed with my education. He said, I should succeed in life through education and that education is a marvelous gift that should not be wasted.

Both my parents and teachers did not agree with me but I told them that,

"I came to school because I want to become rich so now, I have found a way to become rich."

I also threw an African proverb in their face and said "sometimes if a child is pleading for something you need to let him have his way and prove himself wrong in the end".

"Mwana akalilira nyanga ya nsatsi, nsemere imufotere yekha."

"if a child cries for a wooden horn give it to him so it wilts in his hands."

I was out of order, and I knew I was out of order, I figured I had nothing to lose when embarking on my new mission. Therefore, I was still bold and audacious enough to request help to set me on my new journey. So, I told my dad,

"I know you are not happy with me or my decision, but I need you to loan me a cow that will help me get some money to kickstart my business."

My dad was gracious enough to loan me a cow which I sold for K77. With the proceeds I bought salt and then bartered it with groundnuts. I managed to trade salt for a total of 25 bags of groundnuts. I resold this to Admarc for K770 and made quite a profit that enabled me to buy 32 bags of fertilizer and 16 packets of maize seed. Just for perspective, at that time each 50kg bag of fertilizer was K5 meaning that I had quite a lot of money left over.

I rallied my whole family, yes both my parents and brothers, and hired labourers to work on our farm and I gave them one objective...

"Let's farm maize just as I saw it on the Dedza farm".

Of the produce I had earlier, I remained with 1 bucket of groundnuts and instead of eating it I sold it as a snack to-go, sold and measured by the spoon, and made K24 kwacha from the sales. I wondered how I would safely go back with this money to my village, which was, in thoe times, no small amount of money. I decided to buy rice and put it on a bus on my way home. On arrival I sold the rice and even made another profit on it meaning I had transferred the money from Nkhotakota at no cost.

Together with the profits from my Admarc produce sale, I put my resources into my farming costs for that season. As a result of our effort we managed to increase our harvest yield from 4 oxcarts in a year to 63 oxcarts in a year. 1 oxcart is roughly half a ton of corn.

We were now at a level at which I could comfortably say we had overcome hunger. However, I still wondered how could we move from simply being well fed to meeting other daily needs. That's when I ventured into tobacco farming.

I decided to farm burley tobacco, but I had one challenge to surmount. I was not licensed to grow the crop since it was a regulated crop. However, I sold it through other licensed growers and made K1,700. Now compare that to the price of a brand-new Honda bike selling at K900. With this first harvest I concluded that I can be a tobacco farmer after all, and I registered as a licensed farmer. This led to a harvest of 163 bales of barely tobacco from a meager 29 bags in the first year. Then I harvested 1000 bales with proceeds of K23,000 which you can compare to a brand new truck that was selling for K19,000 at the time. So, this was a lot of money!

The transportation and wood businesses

I also ventured into the transportation business and general buying and selling.

I was still yearning for more because of my desire to conquer basic poverty to progressing to something bigger and better and to an improved quality of life. As a result, I became curious at how the developed world became more advanced and developed. I took it upon myself to take a tour and see why. I bought a ticket and carried $5,000 for a short trip.

I made a startling discovery that there are no sales of products requiring further value addition nothing really sold in its raw and unprocessed state. Everything was a finished product meaning that manufacturing was one of their critical keys to their development. I was startled to see Kenyan fashion products in Sweden and I was inspired to add value to our local products hoping for similar prospects. This meant working on fashion handbags and earrings.

Of particular interest to me was the wood industry because I was captivated by the finished wood products and the high-quality furniture that I saw. I therefore set out to buy equipment for wood manufacturing and processing. I thought of our local wood industry and how underdeveloped it was, and to some extent, still is. I knew there was enough forests and wood for similar high-end products. In fact, countries like China import our wood and sell us finished products instead. It seemed a logical venture to me.

However, in my quest to buy the machinery I received a lot of discouragement from the sellers themselves who raised all sorts of questions.

"Who would operate it in Malawi?

Do you even have skilled labor for other tasks in the manufacturing process?

The warranty would be void as soon as it leaves the country, and won't you be wasting your money? "

I insisted that you only die once and chose to respectfully disagree with them. I paid for it and came back to Malawi. On my return I was told that I had to pay storage charges for me to collect it and that once it sold, they cannot hold it free of charge. I was forced to pay with much protest and unhappiness of course.

I was told that the machine I bought was for finishing and that actually I needed a sawmill first. No one in Malawi knew where I could buy this machine and I started a big manhunt, rather machine hunt. My search led me to various furniture companies and one of them called WICO furniture's referred me to a product catalog of a south African supplier. I ordered the machine but once the machine arrived, I was told to pay duty. I hadn't envisioned this as I thought it was a duty-free product. And to my dismay I had to leave it at the border with customs. It stayed for a few months and eventually got rusty. I was advised to plead my case with the Malawi Investment Promotion agency who in turn referred me to the treasury. They took their time and after a few months they eventually waived the duty. But by this time all the blades were rusty. I soon started operating in the Chikangawa forest area and the venture turned out to be quite successful and I used my initial profits from the venture to buy some land in the central region of Malawi.

The story of Blessings Hospital

I intended to use this land for a school but then had some Swedish friends of mine who suggested that I build a hospital. In shock, I said I am no doctor neither do I know how to run a hospital! But they insisted and said they would help me with administrative and ongoing support.

We named the hospital "Blessings Hospital" because we wanted it to be a blessing to the community. We deliberately do not charge market prices so that the poor man in the village can afford our services. With the necessary help we built the hospital in 2001 and started operations in 2002.

I had an interesting experience as we were building the hospital in 2001. I was so passionate about helping people because I was so unsure of my ability to run the hospital that I thought helping the people directly is better. I said if the people are not fed, what will medicines do to them? And I had two ventures. The first was Likuni Phala nutrition project which I did with funding from donors in Sweden. I was offered two full cargo containers of supply but much as it was a good deal I declined it. I told them that it creates a dependency syndrome and I would love something that helps them earn their help and that would automatically create value addition and jobs.

The other thing I tried was to distribute food when the hunger situation got severe. Yes I know it was quite ironic that here I was advocating for food distribution when I earlier declined support on account of creating a dependency syndrome. I used some of my profits and distributed food to 200 people.

I also got some help from a friend of mine Suzie Stevens who gave me $26,000 that I used to buy maize in Tanzania. That was a big mistake because word quickly got out and I ended up giving out food to over 1000 people. Soon I had many people just camp around my house until I deserted my house and ran away to the hospital.

So as the hospital was being built I was grappling with the hunger situation. I still tried to deal with it as much as I could so that I bought Irish potatoes and distributed them to the poor that year. However, it still wasn't enough. Then.... a thought struck me! "If the climate is good and the soil is fertile why don't we irrigate our crops in Malawi generally?" I lamented the situation and resolved to teach the community the benefits of irrigation.

I told my intentions to my colleagues and one of them named "Deputy Gospel" bought the idea. He bought me a drip irrigation system and I started training people in irrigation. After I had taught some people from the surrounding rural community, I put the people to the test and so I was nowhere to be seen for about 1.5 months. This was just to see if they had internalized the learning I gave them. To my dismay they totally forgot everything I taught them, and they too had abandoned the irrigation lessons.

I wondered how I could ensure that people learned and internalized the knowledge to the extent of them implementing this in their daily lives. I thought the best way was to set up a school whereby they could reside on campus for the duration of the studies and allow them to pay a little something.

I had a school in mind and immediately started ploughing streets and marking off areas for the campus. I was already naming everything including the streets even though I didn't have a cent to my name. I simply believed in the word of God which says if you have faith and say to a mountain be removed and cast into the sea, it will move.

Irrigation

Government soon took notice of me and gave me 10 motorized pumps. I had 10 people who were helping me with the work, so I allocated 10 fields, 1 to each of them, to be irrigating and also started some awareness and marketing efforts.

I believe irrigation is key for national development. I think of it as an agricultural backup system especially now in times of climate change and the need for adequate resources and food produce as a nation. The irrigation scheme I have has solar powered pumps that do away with the electricity from the national grid. My projects are in various districts in the central region including Madisi. One of the crops I irrigate is rice. This crop is a good forex earner for Malawi, because Malawi has one of the best rice varieties in the region. It is very aromatic compared to imported rices. The only problem we have is poor quality or no professional processing at all. Our rice is mostly littered with either sand or stone grains. This does not make for a good meal when you accidently grind on a grain of stone while eating. The result is a bad reputation for our rice.

For this reason, I bought rice milling equipment, following one of my trips to China, that sorts, grades, polishes, weighs and packs. It does the whole rice milling process from de husking. It occupies 110m of floor space and spans across 3 floors. This machine really helps to avoid contamination and also to helps in value addition of local produce.

Safi and Mtalimanja Holdings

Safi means "School of agriculture for family independence". This is something that came to fruition a little later than Blessings Hospital. Its model of operation is to invite the local villagers in rural Malawi to learn good and modern agricultural practices including irrigation farming in order to improve their livelihoods.

Local farmers don't always get the full benefits of agricultural advice because the graduates from Lilongwe University of Agriculture and Natural Resources will rarely settle in the rural areas to provide support to farmers. So Safi helps fill this gap by empowering locals with the necessary agricultural knowledge. People have been concerned at how married couples cope with staying away from their family for such long periods of time. But I think of it in just the same way that an illness is treated. People will do all they can to be with their loved ones in hospital by making the necessary adjustments. In the same manner if they are serious about improving their livelihoods, they will make the necessary adjustments to their life. So, they leave their homes and come to the Safi agricultural school and stay in their private accommodation with their spouses. In other situations, the spouse will commute from home to the campus.

The course duration has deliberately been set at 2 years and they graduate with an agricultural diploma. After they graduate, we follow them up with our own extension workers and continue to monitor them and share farming advice with them. The graduates serve as practical examples and local community influencers of good farming practices.

I augmented my irrigation efforts with a Dam. The dam was established in 2012 and in 2019 we upgraded it to 1.5km X500m and 5m deep. Right beside the dam we have established a rice paddy as explained before. The other plantation we have has a banana crop. In addition to this we have an animal feed project so that our operations are self-sustaining once we venture into the rearing of various animals including our current fish farming project. We also think this will help us to earn income from sales of the product.

I am really hoping that this will be a forex earner for the country as we will export to neighboring countries such as Zambia and Mozambique. This concept is now about "teaching people how to fish" because if we give them the fish they will eat and go hungry but if we teach them the skill of fishing, they will fend for themselves after they finish their fish supplies.

Mtalimanja holdings

The culmination of my efforts led to the incorporation of Mtalimanja Holdings Limited (MHL). This is the company that established the rice milling factory which in the year 2015 was touted to be the largest rice milling factory in southern Africa. With an anticipated daily capacity of 200,000 metric tons there is a large potential for export revenue. The company has no less than 400 hectares in various places including Dowa and Nkhotakota where the factory is based. 7000 small holder farmers have been mobilized to exclusively grow rice and we provide them with necessary inputs, extension services and ultimately a market because we buy the crop from them as well.

With the, then, Japanese Ambassador Shuichiro Nishioka saying that "Malawi has the best quality rice in the world and there is need to produce it in huge quantities because it can easily be exported", it can generate, about $500 million a year.

Now, because my system involved training through allocation of land to local farmers, I have at times been questioned on whether or not I want to run a system of feudalism but my rationale for all this is community ownership. I was inspired by the Coca cola company which was started by crowd funding from a community in Atlanta Georgia, who till this day earn a dividend from sales. I think that this company can benefit the local community in a similar way as opposed to feudalism in which the "Lord of the Manor" principally benefits.

I believe there is power in collaboration because if I pick up a handful of dirt and throw it in the air, the handful of dirt will be quickly blown away in the direction of the wind. But, if pick a dirt boulder and hurl it in the air, it will go in the direction I want it and it will go very far. The handful of dirt may have the same mass as the boulder but because it is not integrated or held together and it has no critical mass that can enable it to go farther. The boulder however will go much much farther and that's why working together helps. Because you do much much more!

MHL also invested in a $3million bamboo factory in 2015 along the Kasiya road in Lilongwe which is giving jobs to not less than 70 people. The bamboo factory is producing flooring materials, paint brushes, cutting boards, roofing materials, umbrellas and blinds. The much touted and complained about toothpicks are also being produced. It also intends to export some of its bamboo products. Currently the company is sourcing bamboos from farmers in Lilongwe rural and Mchinji district.

MHL also made investments in Madalitso Food Production and a Sugar Cooperation. in 2012 I also led a group of businessmen who made a major investment in biodiesel technology in Malawi.

I am also building a hotel and a tourist area around the farm and hope this will help to boosting tourism.

A heart to heart, Final words

My final words are that don't fear failure. In Chichewa the saying goes, "Kudziwa njinga ndi kugwa nayo" ("Knowing a bicycle is falling with it") meaning that you can only know how to really ride a bike after falling one or two times, so don't be afraid of falling off your bike in business. Business is a 50:50 game and not all have prospered. You will be deep in the trenches and experience tough moments just as I said.... I have slept in drains along the road before when I was doing buying and selling of sieves.

Change your habits if you are to prosper and learn frugality. You should also value exposure and practical experience because much as education is helpful, the practical experience is invaluable. The relevance and scope of applicability of education is not always maintained and while I have not obtained a formal education, I have been awarded a doctorate degree in entrepreneurship because of the immense value of my practical experience in agricultural farming practices and entrepreneurship in general. I am now able to share my experience with others who have attained a formal education. So please value experience also.

I don't consider myself to be rich but consider myself a mere steward deciding how to help others with the resources, knowledge, and passionate obsessions and burdens that God has given me. Therefore, I want to serve the community through setting systems and discovering how best to do things, such as systems of finance, cooperative arrangements, better administration of various farming and entrepreneurial operations, access to markets, research and development and discovering what the markets need.

I believe that serving your country is not done in just one way such as politics, but it is also about running and being in my own lane and my own field of passion and expertise. I have been invited to join politics by both Americans and Malawians but have asked myself that "between God's office and the people's office which is better?" I am currently in God's office in the mercy department as an ambassador of God, so why should I leave God's office to enter man's office? so currently I am not thinking of joining politics.

The word of God says "guard your heart above all things because out of it comes the issues of life" so I think we should all guard our hearts to ensure we pursue the passions, burdens and obsessions of our hearts. We should channel them into the works of our hands so that we should have a prosperous life.

8

Lilly Alfonso

"Malawi's living legend"

Lilly Alfonso

She is a globally renowned and multi-award-winning Malawian fashion designer.

Lilly Alfonso is the founder of a luxury fashion brand. She is a woman who turned her childhood passion into a growing global brand, she is the CEO & Founder of a fashion and design label named after herself, Lilly Alfonso.

Company

LILLY ALFONSO
Wear It. Feel It.

Countries: Global from Malawi
Achievements

Her creations have been modeled on international runways in

1. Cairo
2. Paris
3. London
4. Milan
5. Kuala Lumpur
6. Amsterdam
7. Sydney &
8. Barcelona

She won the Fashion Malawi Edition (FAME) award in 2010 as Fashion Designer of the year.

In 2019, she was awarded the International Fashion Designer Award in Cairo, Egypt for her contribution to the fashion and creative industry.

Her work has been featured on international media and she has been interviewed by CNN, VOA and BBC.

Lilly's story

I am Lilly Alfonso. I was born in a Family of seven and was named after my grandmother Lilly Panonerethi. For some peculiar reason they did not want to mention my grandma's name so they simply called me "madam". I am very well known in my home township simply as "madam". My dad was the last born of six kids in grandma Lilly's family. I am a second born, also in a family of 6.

My childhood was quite typical of many Malawian childhoods as I grew up in Kanjedza in the usual 2-bedroom houses. And with 6 kids and extra cousins, space was an issue, so the boys would sleep in the sitting room, and girls in the bedroom. Sometimes, quite interestingly, we would swap, just to give the boys a taste of what a bedroom feels like.

I was normally the odd one out in most of the things I did and was unconventional in the way I did them. Mostly, I did them in my own way, whether it is washing dishes or mopping I would just do it differently. As a result, I used to get in trouble a lot.

This was particularly evident with clothes. Because every clothing I had was not good enough for me, I had to do some magic and make it better. So, one time I was bought a new dress and I had to work my magic on it, as it wasn't fitting well on me, or so I thought. And when my mum was taking us to church with our Sunday best, she got the fright of her life!

She shouted, 'church time!'

But to her, not so pleasant, surprise, I had trashed my dress by cutting one side. And, when I did that, somehow I knew I had messed up, so I hid the new dress under my mattress and my mum came and asked,

"where is your new dress?

"I can't find it I have misplaced it"

So, I was told to wear something else. After I wore other clothes, my brother still found the dress and ran to my mum with it. You can imagine the sheer shock and terror in her eyes! So that was the norm for me.

As Lilly narrated her story, she started showing me some of her old pictures where she had been given smart clothes by her parents. In one of them she was in lovely dress which seemed quite normal to me. In another picture she was in her brother's jacket, but true to form, she told me how uncomfortable she was in those 'nice' clothes. She then showed me her Facebook posts of similar pictures and the comments she got from her friends saying

'I remember Madam and I went to the same primary school and Sunday school, we played a lot together, I remember she had her own sense of fashion and I did not understand why, she would always cut pieces of her clothes and sew patches on it, got told off and even got grounded. I remember saying 'Madam has a strange way of dressing' …here she is now an Icon I've never been surprised it's like the feeling of 'finally (it has happened)'.'

Lilly continued narrating her story..... This was a post from a friend whom I had last seen in primary school and I am surprised that even now people say "did you see this?".

but I am grateful for my late Father who used to defend and encourage me. He told my mom that "you know what?", "I think you should stop punishing her, it seems there is something about her that you don't know, I think sometimes you should just pay attention to her and see what she is up to".

That was the greatest gift that daddy gave me and that I carry and cherish to this very day. What I have learnt is that one of the greatest gifts for our children is not what we give them, but what we say to them. I say this because my dad's words encouraged me immensely. I was so young when I hear those words, but that's what has made Lilly Alfonso.

Sometimes if you're not sure of why a child does something, its better to give them a chance and try to understand them instead of just punishing them or saying negative and destructive words to them. This is common in our society because if they are not doing well in school, we tell them "wopanda nzeru" (ignorant, dumb, stupid), you are telling them to believe they are ignorant dumb and stupid.

In fact, the definition and identity of a child is not just in their academic achievements because every child has his own gift. God gave us different gifts and what matters is the very rare ability to see the best in our children and our friends and all those around us.

So, my father's voice always speaks to me and rings in my mind. "snap, snap snap" as Lilly was telling me this story, she was now so engulfed in the memory of her father and the power of his words that she was literally snapping her fingers, and so she continued

'Every time he would say

"believe in yourself"

"Stay put

"Always stand tall

"Never allow people to put you down just because you don't have certain things, always stand tall

And I remember at some point when I was growing up, I liked to stitch and as the fascination grew, I took my mum's sewing machine and made little pieces of cloth, mostly I was making some amendments. I then got tired of it. And tried another thing and failed, then another and several other things, they also failed but every time I went back to my sewing I seemed to find my peace, as if I was in my element, I seemed to have found the real me that comes with life and light all over me, and that strange sense of energy!

Some of the things I tried to do were computer operations, I then studied marketing and then started working in sales and marketing with Minolta and later I worked with Canotech. I was doing relatively well but I did not get the fulfillment I craved. After getting my degree, I felt that the structured work life was not my thing. I seemed to hate structure and rules.

Later, I started following my dream. I started with my mum's sewing machine. She told me that 'you can use this for whatever things you are doing"

I then opened a small shop on a veranda. I closed it and opened it again. Then things started changing and I started getting attention. But until then I didn't know that I had strength in designing. I also thought it was my private hoppy a thing that would help me pass time.

So, my tailoring shop was called Lilly's creations, it did not set off at once, so I combined my work with interior designing coz I am also good at that. Because of the challenges I was experiencing I thought I should not just idle around but started learning carpentry so there you have it! I am also a carpenter!

..... As she narrated this she paused and confessed she was not proud of the name she is about to mention, then she continued

'I called the business "Natural designs and décor'

then she laughed at herself and I was wondering why she laughed. She then confessed that

'I called it natural because its not something I went to school for and some friend of mine said "chi name ichi its too long bwanji?' "this big name of yours why is it too long and uninspired".

Then she laughed again, and I caught her humor....

'So later on, I created the business called "Lilly Alfonso Creations" which was a combination of the two businesses. When I cam to Lilongwe I opened my interior designing shop and clients were buying furniture, hiring me to work on their homes and lodges. But I realized that I am spending a lot of time to finish the projects and people were not paying in time. So, I put more effort in the fashion and designing side.

Whilst I did that, I won an award of the Fashion Malawi Edition (FAME) 2010 as best designer under the award "Fashion Designer of the Year". In 2011 I went to Italy to study and understand more about the fashion business. It just got into my system and I never stopped and kept pushing and pushing and pushing.

Soon I was getting more recognition and exposure and the invitations for interviews kept on coming and coming and before I knew it, I was called by the BBC, VOA and then CNN and that just opened more doors for more media houses like Map Africa and it led to greater online coverage.

Once the publicity came in, I thought to myself why I could not do more with it than just my business so that I can even help others beyond me and even my own country. Why can't I do something that changes people's mindset? Why can't I change how things are done and how people think. The analogy is that most people are like those that stand before a river, fearful and paralyzed by people's voices that say "you will drown". I ask myself why can't I be the one to jump? Why can't I swim to the other side and create a bridge? Why can't I inspire others through fashion?

The challenges

I think the biggest challenge in Malawi is the mindset that something cannot be done. People want and desire to see good things done but the support structure is not there in terms of both moral and financial support. What actually happens is that people will tell you that "you can't do that coz its not possible".

At the same time, you need to pay your rent and bills, and to survive. When you think of all the problems you have it's not just about one or two variables. It's not the money or the moral support alone. It's more about the mindset, because the mind is where our greatest battles lie. Its not about not going to the best fashion school or not having business capital or the market. It's about how we think on a day to day basis.

I believe we need to change our mindset to aspire for more, to hold ourselves more accountable, to think of unique businesses and not to just follow the crowd because its safe, we need to think of investing in what we believe in. We also need to have more faith in ourselves as a people and a nationality and even as a race. We should not look down upon ourselves but believe that we also have a lot to offer the world. Unfortunately, we may not be too appreciated or treated equally around the world. But we need to see the value in ourselves because when God created all of us, he gave us all unique gifts but many of us have not used our gifts because we hear the global narrative that we're not good enough or have nothing good to offer to the world.

The key is to invest in our passion and do what our hearts love most.

If we invest into our passion how far can we really go? But if its work, as long as the hours are up, you're off to the house because you're not doing it with your heart. But you're forgetting that whatever you put your hands to it produces fruit whether at work or at home in your area of passion.

So, for me, when I try to think about the challenges I have gone through, I try to focus on the solutions and what I can do about the situations I am in.

I also benefited from the exposure I was getting, and I soon realized I needed to be agile in the way I handle customers and interact with business contacts. It's the subtle things like how you speak, reach out and persuade others. You quickly learn that I need to change this, and I need to change that.

The distribution channels are also something I had to deal with. How would I get my product to market? I had to learn and stumble along the way starting from Facebook, how would I provide a bespoke product to someone I had never met? How do I make payment systems that work for such a closed up and undeveloped financial system. Which systems do I use? Unfortunately, most of our banks stick to the traditional payment methods which are totally dangerous such as getting swift codes and routing numbers. Then I tried to set up a website and payment system which failed to work at first.

How do I ship my products when the shipping costs more than the products? How do I deal with competition locally? and also copy cats from around the world who sell at a fraction of the cost?

But I had to think outside the box and surmount all those challenges. And the outcome of this was establishment and a growing customer base. Now I have customers all over the world including Italy, the Americas and Europe. I have modelled my creations on international runways in Cairo, Paris, London, Milan, Kuala Lumpur, Amsterdam, Sydney and Barcelona.

In 2019 I was also awarded the International Fashion Designer Award in Cairo Egypt for my contribution to the fashion and creative industry.

Under my fashion label, I produce ready to wear for both women and men under sub labels; LAwomann, LAmann and the newly launched LAsport

I asked her whether or not there is a spiritual side to her creativity and if she sees God in what she does. Her answer was intriguing.

'One thing that has driven me is the question of 'how can I make a lasting impact and do something that outlives me?

I thought of the impact I have in fashion and wondering how this can be realized. I said 'I create 30 designs a day and even more designs if I have time, would this outlive me? No, fashion is ever changing, and it comes and goes. I thought if I am successful so what next? I was even tempted to set up outside the country, so I went to Turkey and few other countries in 2014 and wanted to find out how differently they do things. I saw that yes, they have better equipment but for the most part the people are just like us in the way they do things, they have the same hands and same head and limbs. I wondered what benefit I would have if I set up there. I thought how would my country benefit if the revenue flows are not coming back home? Even if I have all the money and publicity but how does that fulfil me? How would I succeed alone and not inspire the young girls and the women back in my country?

I then decided that I needed to set up home in Malawi, I turned to my team and told them that we have to set up here. Even if it takes us longer but its my duty to help others with my gift. The questions I had in my mind are

'why God am I here?

'why was I born here in this hostile and limited environment, why have I achieved what I have achieved?

Then I said 'Lord you're telling me why you gave me this gift and what I am going to do with it and if you're not telling me then you're going to guide me to achieve whatever you want me to achieve. If you knew I am done here, and you want me to be somewhere you would have easily let me be born there and not here. So you have a bigger reason why I was born here. I am going through these challenges and limitations so help me. So God told me "stay, stay there"

I continued to face challenges, but God said "Stay"

I cried out to God and say things are not moving but God said "Stay there"

No one was giving me attention at some point, but God said "Stay there"

But the bottom line is that because I gave my life to God to guide me that's why I have become successful and why I am what I am to-day. I may not be considered successful in other people's eyes, but I have become successful spiritually and whatever I do I have learned to understand that I have a purpose to fulfil.

This purpose has led to so many people around the world asking how is it you are doing what you are doing. Come and please talk to our women. These are CEO's in the corporate world who want to learn lessons in resilience and success. I am called to various high-level conventions such as Lionesses of Africa. All this however, happens under the blind eye of my own community that seems unconcerned of my activity.

But out of my own initiative I share the same secrets to local rural women as I do to the CEO's.

So you need to be driven by purpose because many people are going the direction of the crowd that says we need to do things this way or go that way.. Because I want people to know they have value and they can do something of worth.

Even if people locally do not value my contribution, I still continue doing it and I get encouraged with BBC and CNN who are coming back to follow up on my progress.

Because of this passion I came up with what I call the 100-year plan whereby I have a program that invests in children. I cannot change the mindset of adults, but I can shape the thinking of young people. I train young people in fashion designing and business skills. I bring them in class daily by showing them my work. I inspire them and they then see themselves through my eyes. So, I give them clear images of my humble beginnings. I tell them to practice what they are doing and show them areas where they ought to concentrate on.

Currently, my students are showing their works around the world including Australia. I am telling people that If you buy a piece of Lilly Alfonso you are investing in this project of training young people. So, I hate this mindset of begging, of "give me this because I have this and that project". People must see the value in you. So, it's our duty to create change but how do we do it? Do it the right way so people will benefit, and that people will learn as they see me do.

The other thing I believe in is the fact that you cannot walk alone. And at Lilly Alfonso there is a collaborative culture.

I also teach my students to find their purpose in life. They also need to understand that

"what is success?"

"what is success?"

"is it because I have money in the bank?

"is success the fact that everyone knows Lilly Alfonso

I don't want to die in regret, I don't want to be rich and when I am going, I am complaining why I didn't do this and why am I going?

If it's my time I should say well and good, don't cry for me, I have set up this and that and my family is taken care of. My life does not end here. But when many people are dying, they complain, I have this and that, I wish I did this.

I believe I have a purpose. My purpose is to make sure that people have seen the light. If God gave you the gift of writing use it well, if God gave me the gift of designing let me use it to reach out to people and tell them they too can achieve things in life. That's why the 100-year plan is my personal passion that helps me achieve this path by fostering mindset change, educating and training, inspiring and motivating.

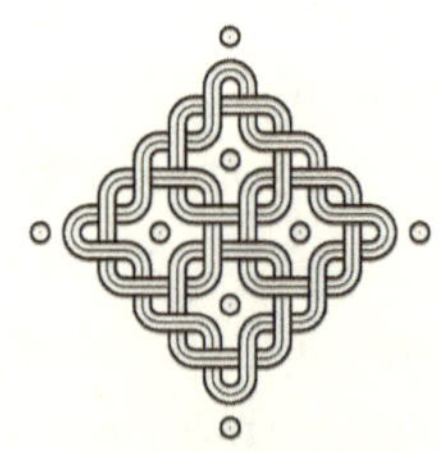

9

Ngabaghila Chatata

"The woman who found a future in her passion"

Ngabaghila Chatata

Ngabaghila is the Managing Director of Thanthwe Enterprises and co-founder with her husband Dziko Chatata.

They started Thanthwe with personal savings from their jobs and focused on climate smart agriculture technologies including greenhouse and drip irrigation technologies and are now making strides in agro-processing.

Thanthwe is driven by its motto: "Following Passion, Feeding the Nation".

Fast facts

Date of Birth   8 June 1979
Company

Countries   Malawi
Achievements
She has obtained recognition both locally and regionally

1. She won the "Entrepreneur of the Year" Award from the Small and Medium Enterprises Development Institute
2. She won the "Regional Farmer Award" from the Reginal Universities Forum for Capacity Building Agriculture.
3. Creation of an Agribusiness incubation hub

4. She is an alumni of the US Embassy supported African Women Entrepreneurship Programme for 2016
5. She served as Chairperson of the Lilongwe Horticultural Farmers Cooperative
6. She serves and served on various boards including Farmers Union of Malawi and Welthungerhilfe.
7. Her work has been featured on international media and has been interviewed by the BBC.

Who am I?

Ngabaghila Chatata is my name, I am the sixth born in a family of 8 children comprising 5 girls and 3 boys. My father was an accountant at the Agricultural Development Cooperation of Malawi while my mom was a stay at home mom.

The name Ngabaghila, is pronounced "Ngawayira" and it means "I have been given too good a gift for which I am underserving". It is a name that talks of the undeserved grace and favor of God.

I am married to Dziko Chatata my college sweetheart whom I met at Chancellor college a constituent college of the University of Malawi. He was doing a Bachelor of Science while I was pursuing a Social Science Degree. We graduated in 2002 and got married in 2003.

I am a mother of 2 boys and 2 girls. The first is Wakisa, a girl , followed by Thanga, also a girl and then two boys Joshua and Isaac.

I was born in the Malawian city of Blantyre, in an area called Maone and did my primary school education at Chichiri Primary School, my secondary school education at Henry Henderson Institute, and my tertiary education at Chancellor college as indicated earlier.

In my earlier days I would help my mom in our vegetable garden and she would give me my own yard and seeds for me to plant and grow. I would grow various vegetables on my own including corn. However, it was mostly a hobby that I was passionate about and for which I remained passionate until I grew up.

I lost my dad in 1996 when I was in form 3 of secondary school education, but fortunately my elder sister, Faggy, bless her soul, assumed the role of caretaker and ensured that we got an education and the needs of the home.

How it all began

I realized over time that I am a person who loves dealing with complexity and random and nonlinear things. I like to connect the dots and make sense of things.

After my college graduation I joined the Malawi civil service by working with the Malawi Government as a Data Officer for only 7 months. I then moved on to an organization called C-Code for about 4 months before joining Care international, ActionAid, and WaterAid before moving to head WES-Netwok. I worked in the areas of urban Governance, policy and advocacy, economic empowerment of women and youth, community mobilization, street kids and commercial sex-workers' rehabilitation

Together with my husband, we discovered that we both have a passion for farming and decided to go into commercial farming. We also felt financially insecure because we were both working on a contract basis with our respective employers. In response to our concerns we thought we ought to do something as an exit strategy that would help us be more financially stable. As we discussed our family vision, the conversation moved into wondering about "what would be a wise investment for us?"

We thought we could do what we both loved and not invest in our dream cars just yet and discovered that we both shared a passion for farming. We started researching about irrigation agriculture and related practices. I think our communication was quite good and this allowed us to share our dreams with each other and we even had a vision board where we would not only talk, but also write about our dreams. This greatly helped us to put our points across. There were many occasions in which both of us tried to explain what the other had said and we continuously corrected each other. In an attempt to better communicate we literally drew what we meant to say to avoid misunderstanding each other. And indeed, we had to correct each other and "re-draw" our concepts again and again.

We continued to follow our passion, but time was soon running out as years passed by. We talked and talked until 2010 when we made a radical family decision. We chose to relocate from the urban low density and prestigious housing location in Area 10 in Lilongwe to the farm that we had bought way back in 2004. Yes, to the farm! People thought we had gone bonkers as this was a very unusual thing to do.

However, our passion was consuming us. We felt that Malawi as a nation was not really creating wealth for its citizens and were concerned that most of our fruits and vegetables were all imported into our major retail shops. And so we thought our farming activities could achieve the much-touted import substitution even though on a small scale. Our dream was and still is "to have a Malawi that can grow, process and export high value agricultural produce".

We also discovered that Malawians are now more exposed to various types of cuisine and are demanding more high-quality products. Naturally, we saw this as a business opportunity.

The farm we moved to was on a plot of land on which nothing much grew. It was a sandy piece of land that was not really fertile and had little to no crops on it. For some reason we still decided to buy the land in the hopes of professional reclamation. So, we bought 6 acres of land and started applying manure to the land, all the while being mocked by the neighbors and onlookers that constantly asked "who would buy such infertile land?"

We managed to start farming on the reclaimed portions of land, and this remains an ongoing task. We decided to mind our family spending and adopt austerity measures and therefore could not spend lavishly on most of our needs.

When I was working with my last employer, I discovered that I am working very hard so that if this effort was exerted into my own things then I could eventually pay myself. I wondered why I could not achieve the same objective, work for myself and be my own boss. Fortunately, my husband was quite understanding and supportive of my rationale and I quit my job to fully concentrate on our business and passion. It was a hard decision to make but it was one I felt was necessary and in line with our family vision. In fact we both thought of quitting but I guess I was the bolder one, bold enough to actually take the leap of faith. We also agreed that my skill sets were the ones that the business requires at start up level.

I was very hands on with the business and would interact a lot with the customers. I took orders, prepared them and delivered them myself. This helped me get an understanding of the business so that as we grew, I am still able to understand the business even though I may not be doing those exact tasks. It helps me know if things are going on well or not and if I need to make any changes to weaknesses I observe in the business.

I must admit I had to battle a bit of a cultural challenge with my staff. They were mostly workers from surrounding villages, and they found it very difficult to accept that a 'woman' is the overall boss of the farm. They would always try to second guess me, by saying *"Koma abambo akuti titere" ("but your husband says we should do this")*. However, I would always emphasize my point until they followed my instruction. Fortunately, my husband would also refer them to my final comments as well, so this type of support greatly helped. Finally, they began to realize and respect my role as the overall in charge responsible for the farm operations and that "abambo" "the man of the house" was happy to place everything under my care and supervision.

I have learned to approach business as a professional and not as a woman because society takes every opportunity to remind you that you are a woman. It tries to pull you down because of it, but when it realizes you are capable as men, society just has to work with you in your own right as a professional. So, I am very lucky to have a husband who understands and respects me as a professional and a leader in my own right. I later employed my husband as the operations Manager, and he does a great job,... I'm definitely not firing him any time soon.

At the beginning of our operations we stumbled on the greenhouse technology. We started doing a bit of research into greenhouse science and drip irrigation. We started with setting up a local greenhouse, but it only lasted for 3 years because of the materials used which was the normal plastic on the market and local timber. As the business grew our single greenhouse could not meet the demand because we were only farming on a quarter acre. This prompted us to think of expanding and we thought we could apply for a grant from the Business Linkage

Fund, a project by the Ministry of Trade that is funded by the African Development Bank. We were told to source our own materials and we would be given a matching grant. So, we started with our own contribution but over time we estimate that we contributed more than what was requested from our own resources.

We later researched who the key players and suppliers are on the global market and we discovered an Israeli company that is into this technology. We not only sourced materials from them, but they nominated us to be their agents in Malawi, which is what we also currently do.

After the successful grant application process, we expanded from a quarter acre to 6 acres with 7 greenhouses, from, initially, only 1. On receipt of the construction materials we assembled them ourselves without necessary professional supplier help as would be for other sales that they make. They even commended us for a very well-done installation.

As part of our growth we are now setting up a factory for greenhouse production in addition to a factory for hibiscus products. The factories are tailored to the nature of our operations and products.

We started with a borehole but later dug another one and installed overhead tanks with a large capacity enough for the drip irrigation operations. This technology reduces conventional water usage by 90%

We have always wanted to share our knowledge, and therefore we started opening our gates to the community. However, even though our doors were open to the public we noticed that many of these people never really implemented what they learnt. We discovered that we were just a form of entertainment for them, and they simply came to be amused. Every Jim and Jack who had nothing to do but loiter around would come to us. This meant while I was doing the hard work of sharing my passion, they were literally wasting my time for nothing. We decided to put an end to this and introduced paid visits for a price of about $7 per head.

This immediately screened out the "undesirables" who saw us mere entertainment and a pastime. We now had serious visitors who were ready to pay something to obtain valuable knowledge. It's just a token but even though small, it pushes our visitors to want to both learn something and implement it so that they know their investment was worthwhile.

This has now allowed us to be a proper agribusiness incubator because we now get only interested persons passing through our doors. We have now managed to train about 3000 youth and women plus smallholder farmers through our program, but more through the consultations that we do with UN organizations. One of the things I try to do is to challenge the status quo of farming in Malawi. I try to push this mindset into people and I always ask them why they are doing what they do in the manner they do it. Most of the time I get responses such as

"It's the way it's always been done"

"That's how my father used to do it" or the classic

"That's how we do it in this area"

Over time, I challenge them to see the value in modern farming methods that can be employed in the horticulture business. Hopefully, we will be able to impact many people to adopt modern farming methods such as the greenhouse technology. I advise the youth that if they can find their niche and be creative they can prosper.

We take pride in changing these mindsets and in training as many people as possible because we have no problem in sharing our knowledge through training and we believe that there is more than enough space for more players in the Malawi market.

Challenges

Our journey has not been without its challenges. In fact they were many, but I believe that the biggest was the access to finance for us as new entrepreneurs. The formal banking sector is reluctant to support unproven and unknown small and medium enterprises and they make the conditions for borrowing very stringent which inherently limits access to finance. The other challenge we faced was a lack of knowledge of alternative financing channels such as those I ultimately used to source our matching grant.

I also battled with a largely unskilled workforce and it was a challenge for me to find the right skills for various aspects of the business. For example, in the beginning I had to use a part time accountant as I could not immediately employ a full-time accountant. But as time passed, I was now able to engage the necessary skill set and at the right cost. I also had to work on a business strategy, so we take deliberate steps to grow the business. I have since used various consultants on my farm and currently I have two consultants who have committed to assist me on some current plans.

I think that at the beginning, there was some planning but as the business grew, overtime things changed requiring more contemporary solutions. I believe that with better planning, many growing businesses can definitely do better.

Achievements and establishment

As the business grew, we managed to achieve a few things and we started winning awards and have generally gained recognition in the country and beyond our borders. As a result of this we won the "Entrepreneur of the Year" Award from the Small and Medium Enterprises Development Institute Entrepreneur award in 2017. In the same year I won the "Regional Farmer Award" from the Reginal Universities Forum for Capacity Building Agriculture. In fact, I got these two awards on the very same day and I had to juggle two events without disappointing those who had invited me.

We are now more established and stable than when first began. And we have various farm produce that includes, cucumber, melons, sweet peppers (red and green peppers), Hibiscus products such as our herbal tea, juice and even jam.

We also grow various herbs including rosemary, mint, thyme and coriander. We have cherry tomatoes, and some of the fruits we have are mangoes, pawpawdilla and asparagus. On the animal husbandry side, we have a piggery and we rear chickens.

We have also been instrumental in the establishment of what is called the Lilongwe Horticulture Farmers Cooperative and have set up an agriculture incubation hub providing training for local farmers and we are soon planning to open offices for this new organization in the central business district of Lilongwe. We enroll interns on this program who are given hands-on training on various aspects of greenhouse farming. Under this program we provide inputs to farmers to kickstart their farming and agripreneurial journey.

Hopes for the future

Lastly, we have a few hopes and aspirations for the future. We hope to establish an agro-processing plant and wouldn't it be wonderful if we were to have the largest agro-processing plant in the Southern Africa? That's our dream! Because just like most of Africa, Malawian farmers face challenges with market access due to poor roads and the long distances we have to travel to reach markets, which leads to high post-harvest losses leading to farmers losing essential income. To help tackle this challenge, we are planning to become a produce aggregator to enable individual horticulture farmers to take their farm produce to Thanthwe for processing and/or packaging to make the products more competitive and therefore reduce post-harvest losses.

We also wish to grow into a proper agri-hub with better training resources, facilities and infrastructure.

I am passionate about training because I don't want farmers to struggle the way I did, because we had no role models to learn from. As novices we paid a high price due to trial and errors and going backwards and forwards. But I believe that a better Malawi is a Malawi for all. We would like to improve the current farming methods, pushing the limits of what is possible in Malawi and challenging, influencing and changing the cultural norms and limits of what is possible. And as we do this, we want to continue investing in research and advocacy at our own level. So, where we have an opportunity to interact with the Malawi government, we provide our thoughts and input into various programs and policies that are being drawn up as our contribution to the development of Malawi. We truly hope that we can be a catalyst for meaningful change in Malawi!

IO

Dingase Tewete

"Afana o phusha",

"The one who presses and pushes on"

Dingase is the Founder and Managing Director of Kombeza Foods. A local foods and dairy company with operations starting in Blantyre Malawi. She started her company after her passion for business was infused with a mother's love to care for her nursing child. Her dissatisfaction with a lack of local baby foods launched her into the baby foods business while her passion to simply help out her parent's dairy business resulted in her mother persuading her into the dairy products business.

Hers is a fascinating story, not only because of what she has achieved but also how relatable she is to all of us. Listen to her carefully, as she shares her journey of how an ordinary person, like you and I, can make an impact in business and society at a large!

Fast facts

Company: Kombeza foods

Countries   Malawi

Education   Masters in Business Administration (MBA)
Bachelor of Business Administration and Management

Who I am

I am Dingase Tewete, currently a mother of 2 and am married to Grey Tewete. I studied a management Degree at the Malawi College of Accountancy and later pursued a Master's in Business Administration Degree with the Eastern and Southern African Management Institute.

I worked with KPMG as an auditor before joining the college of Medicine as Deputy Administrator of the Blantyre Malaria Project having worked with them from 2011 through 2019, when after founding Kombeza Foods in 2018, I had to leave full time employment once my business got established a year later.

How it all began

I think I have always been inspired to do entrepreneurship by my parents who were themselves avid entrepreneurs and especially my mum who specially inspired me as a female entrepreneur. I think this passion showed up in my youth as I tried to do various things on my own. However, I believe I might have lost this passion as I pursued my education, but sure enough the passion was re-ignited especially in early 2015 where I started doing my own research, and also, from deliberately following other entrepreneurs.

One way in which I did this was attending the Pitch Night forums which had recently started and was showcasing other entrepreneurs who had started in business and how they succeeded. I was especially inspired by young entrepreneurs who were making it in business.

On one of the Pitch Nights there was the late Sidik Mia who talked of how he ventured into business by moving out of the trucking business and buying cows after selling his trucks. After a while, he grew his herd to 30,000 cows and the quality was one of the best in Southern Africa, and the money he was making was quite interesting as it really rewarded the risk he initially took.

But what really caught my attention was his bemoaning of the "trading culture" in Malawi as opposed to the "producing" culture. He said that most of our business activity in Malawi, is simply trading without producing anything. And when we trade there is no control over the business and supply chain meaning that you are more dependent on external dynamics of the supply chain so that a disruption in the chain can even spell doom for your business.

He challenged us to "start producing things" and said to just go into the shops and see what we locally produce and what we import as a nation and if we are looking for a business to do, we should "start from there".

Ignited with passion, if not incited with anger!, I went into Shoprite and looked at what was on the shelves. Incidentally I was nursing my 6 month daughter and naturally I was interested in baby foods. What I observed at the time was that our shelves were stocked with imported brands opposed to local brands and it was the imported brands that were selling like hotcakes off the shelves. I went to other shops and discovered a similar trend and that there are few or no local brands in the baby porridge product line.

I decided to venture into this baby porridge product and to even start with my own child. And, fueled by a mothers love, I did a lot of research on the types of porridge, normal and instant, what was happening in other countries, and so on and so forth. Through this research I stumbled upon a 1984 government recipe which I started practicing at home. I started sharing my porridge at work and giving it to friends, and later I went to the Bvumbwe Research station to get the nutrient content properly analysed.

However, the effect of this porridge or "phala" in the Chichewa language was the "licking and scraping effect" a lot like "wiping the plate with your finger" and "licking the porridge off your finger". Even with a spoon people would "wipe it clean". And in Chichewa this is called "ku kombeza". So this is how the name "Kombeza" started, meaning "it's so delicious that mukombeza!" (you will kombeza and "wipe the plate clean").

I continued with the business for another 8 months or so and still researched into the making of the product. Because the key ingredient was cassava flour, I looked at how we could grow the cassava plant as part of our value chain because it started getting very expensive. I got seed from Bunda College and planted 2 hectares of cassava in the northern region of Malawi in my Dad's home. I kept on patronizing the Pitch nights, meeting entrepreneurs and doing research and this emboldened me that indeed I can make it.

Unfortunately there is not much literature about our seasoned entrepreneurs because it's in bits and pieces, shared by a reporter here, and a reporter there making the information all very scanty. So, I made an effort to meet them and I met for example Mark Kastsonga, Thom Mpinganjira and many others. However, what I also enjoyed the most was meeting the young ones, the unknowns and the underdogs, and seeing what they were doing and the income they were making.

What made me stop going to Pitch Night was the 1 year anniversary where they brought in the first entrepreneurs to pitch and share their success stories. On this event there was Nomsa Chikowi and Itaye Chidzero. These guys had moved from doing nothing to raking in several millions. This pushed me to be indignant and ask myself "what am I doing?"

I said to myself "I will not come here until I do something tangible and on point". I thought I had been inspired enough and done enough research and all I now needed was action.

I went home but unfortunately still had to wait for the cassava to mature and as I waited my parents, bought some dairy cows as part of their own business which was calming and rewarding at the same time. As they continued in their business other challenges crept in which manifested when the cows were in their home Khola (kraal) such as failure to sell the produce whenever they are late to deliver because it could not be bought or when they could not buy it on a public holiday. So my mom said "why don't you do something with the milk when it's not bought? Coz the place that buys this milk also does dairy products like cheese and yoghurt. Since you are an entrepreneur surely you can think of something with this left over milk".

I was reluctant at the thought of this because I was not a milk person but, when one day they brought me over 150 liters of left over milk, and a similar quantity the next day, it really hit me that I really needed to do something with this milk. And moved by how my mom implored me (you know how mothers push the right button's just because they know you so well!), moved by the extent of trouble, inconvenience and waste they were experiencing, I decided to "help them" in a way.

I did a bit of my own research into milk production and spoke to my friends about milk and yoghurt production. I eventually found some-one who came to show me even though he himself was a layman so I ended up relying on internet videos that helped me become effectively "self-taught". And with so much trial and error and many "porridge like" yoghurts, I finally got it right.

Once I thought I got it right I also started with my work place. And gave them several samples to taste. Perhaps they "caught on" that they were now as good as human "guinea pigs" and soon they started saying "we like it but we're tired of just tasting perhaps you should start selling it to us". Though they were my human guinea pigs, the good thing is that they like it.

When they started saying this, I knew that they were now ready to become customers and the first time I "sold" the yoghurt, I took 17 bottles and people were so very happy that they bought all 17 bottles. There was no name to it and they would just taste and buy it. And that's how I started in my business. Every time we had leftover milk I made yoghurt until it hit me and I realized that "this is a potential business" and one that I should take seriously so it becomes more steady and for it to meet the increasing demand.

I spoke to my husband about it, and we agreed to go for further training I asked my friend Kenrin who had been helping me from the very beginning with yoghurt ingredients and she gave me a few pointers of people who were training anyone producing at least 5,000 liters... but we could only sell around 150 liters on our good days, with the normal capacity ranging from 20 to 100 liters. However, further pointers later led me to go for yoghurt training in South Africa.

At the time, I was expecting my second born and setting up the business was becoming more labor intensive meaning that I needed help with the various processes of delivery, sales and production. And so I found 3 people placing two in sales and 1 in production. But we had another dilemma, I needed a product name, I thought of various names but the name that kept coming is "Kombeza" because it had the same effect. People wiped their bottles and cups clean, I argued with the printers and others about the name. They said it's not a good name, its not professional, try "creamy youghurt" or "creamy foods" creamy this and creamy that, but I said "Hey it's my product and it's my name" so it was settled, I called the yoghurt "Kombeza".

Regarding the bottle size? As I decided not to belabor myself with filling many small bottles of 250 mls each its better I pack 100 1 liter bottles rather than 400 smaller bottles. So our virgin market was?.... You guessed it, our workplaces "Old mutual" for my husband and the "Queen Elizabeth Central hospital" ("Queens") where my work place was located.

Soon, I was approached by a friend who told me of a growth accelerator program and I thought of applying for it. I was successful but one of the conditions of the grant was that one of the owners should be full time in the business. So we made the difficult decision and I quit my job. At that time we were at about 300 liters a day from 80 liters a day and projecting about 400 liters by the end of the year. But the products became quite popular very very quickly, so much so that by the end of the year we were already at 1,000 liters a day, and while initially, we were making daily sales of about K200,000 we grew to about K1,000,000 daily. It was clear that we needed focus on this business and in December 2018, we decided that I leave employment.

The grant also meant that I undergo some 6 weeks of training. This meant I had to apply for leave from work. I applied for leave and, "thank heavens", they allowed me to attend!

Growing the business and related challenges

In May of 2019, I left work and went full time into the business. By then, I had received a $40,000 grant meant for buying equipment to increase capacity to $1,000 liters but we repurposed it because we were already achieving this capacity manually and we then decided to invest in our factory and to later source additional finance for even larger equipment.

We struggled to get financing because the cost was too high with both murderous and suicidal rates of about 35% per annum! And even when we found a financier they wanted us to give them collateral. And even when we did have collateral, it was short of the necessary collateral amount. In one scenario they said that the collateral we put up is not good because it was a personal house and should we fail to pay we would become homeless. So, the long and short of it, is that we failed to get financing and just grew on our own with internal resources.

We continued to grow organically, slowly, but fairly well so much so that in March 2020 we were in Shoprite and by the end of the year, we were in a local retail chain. But we were only given 1 shop, and also, the shop was in Lilongwe while our operations are domiciled in Blantyre so I hope to get more shops soon after further engagement with them and other local shops. Another shop was then given to us in Mzuzu.

This challenge led us to be ingenious and creative. We set up a local distribution channel and from the very beginning we have been having "boot sales", straight from the trunks of our cars. We first had only 2 cars and they basically started their own street selling business started. We started at our workplaces Queens and Old mutual and they would also go to other locations such as Limbe.

Soon, others would come with their own vehicles and ask to start selling our products on the streets and Lilongwe was the next city, followed by Zomba. We did not have many vehicles because just like the "ice cream bus" concept, it moves around and makes sales. However, the Lilongwe opportunity was quite a good one because one distributor started with 5 vehicles and we agreed to brand them "Kombeza" and sent him 1,000 litres. But this was sold in just 2 days... We continue to face challenges with the street business because of heat and spoilage so we largely focus on shops and offices at the moment. I am hoping that soon this will be found in our international and local hotels as a local delicacy we can all show case.

Other challenges arise due to unreliable power supply which is devastating for this "fresh food" business because a lot of wastage of product happens and it slows down production. When power goes off we can't even buy the milk in the first place since we can't store it.

We also experience problems with quality packaging and we look forward to more affordable and trendy packaging too in Malawi because at the moment, we are yet to have high quality and affordable packaging.

Hopes for the future

Soon we think we will be producing about 6,000 liters a day, and we hope to make strides with a recent business acceleration donation we have received. We think the support we are getting from donors is because of the passion we have which is almost an obsession that is quite contagious.

When we start sharing our dream we infuse the vision in them and they are confident to walk this journey with us. Especially when we demonstrate to them what we have already done and how far we have come. As a result of this, we have got another donation of K160,000,000 meant for business growth.

We want to be the company with the best locally produced products and also to diversify into other dairy products such as cheeses and so on.

We think our brand is strong and will continue to be strong. It is a local name and it is instantly recognized. It smacks of patriotism too! In fact the name Kombeza is well received by locals when we interact with them and ask them about our product. So much so that this success came with a challenge of counterfeiting, with others selling their yoghurts in the name of Kombeza.

The time we set up in business we saw a mushrooming of other yoghurt business and you could find people complaining about the product, but little did they know that they bought a counterfeit. However, we are happy that now this name is replacing the "English" name of yoghurt because if you ask the locals about yoghurt they won't answer you, they will only understand you when you say "I am looking for Kombeza". So we remain hopeful and very encouraged that we will do well if we continue to work hard.

And about working hard, I am grateful to have such a dedicated team, they put in their all, and they understand the vision. In fact we proudly call ourselves "afana o'pusha" (guys who push and press on"). This is just to infuse a hard working spirit in all of us. But above all, we all trust in the grace of God and through our morning devotions we commit everything we do into God's hands as we trust for further growth.

However, I think we need to work on our distribution model so we make the product readily available in the various districts and do it in a manner that is socially responsible. We think the distributorship model is socially responsible because we provide a living for people who participate in the street business and in the very local areas. We think we are giving them their own "small businesses", a sense of independence and dignity, and a livelihood.

I also think that there is need for degree courses that focus on food production and also continuous learning of current trends so that as things improve and consumer trends change we can easily meet their needs. This is something that could help us.

Final words?

When all is said and done, I think I have come a long way and there are a lot of lessons I have learnt along the way such as how to do businesses, lessons around processes such as sales but in all that we are doing, we are striving for excellence and I am calling upon my staff to have a similar mindset of excellence, because sometimes in business we can easily become complacent to think that sales will just come on their own.

Sometimes we use financial constraints as an excuse for neglecting quality but quality is not only about having enough, its about doing the best with what you have, and it' not just about the taste alone but the whole experience of the both taste and the packaging and also the memorable experience the product leaves behind.

It's about understanding your customer and understand their needs, we want to connect with them and leave them with a good feeling about our product....Yes, the Kombeza effect of wiping the cup clean and wanting more! This, I believe, will bring us loyal and repeat customers. I truly hope that we will always strive for excellence in all we do!

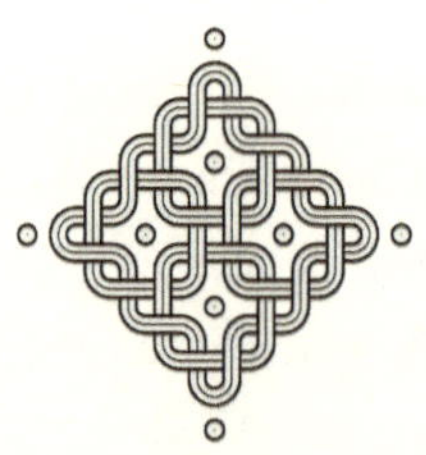

Towera Jalakasi

"The lady who did not see 'the entrepreneur in her" when others did"

Towera has worked for various organizations locally and internationally, providing business counselling and consulting services. Towera is a leader in the field of SME development and a CEO of two organisations, The first is "Tools for Enterprise & Education Consultants" where she specializes in refining and developing businesses and market opportunities as well as brokering relevant partnership solutions in the business and finance sector.

With a degree in food and nutrition, her ingenuity nourishes the nation through her natural fruit juices and organic products through "Naturals Limited", the second organisation she founded.

While she was busy tutoring entrepreneurs, she was oblivious to the fact that she had a potential business until someone pointed this out to her. Soon, she started living the message she was preaching, and started adding value both to herself and those around her.

Towera started from a home garage and has now grown her business into a nationwide operation so that from a sole trader, she now runs a successful family owned business.

She has met several challenges along the way and learned how to overcome them by re-inventing herself and always thinking of growing the potential in her business.

Fast facts

Year of Birth   1967
Company
Naturals Limited
Tools for enterprise and education consultants
Countries   Malawi
Education
Bachelor of Science in Education - Food and nutrition
Advanced Diploma in Business Counselling   and consulting
Achievements
Towera heads a women's investment cooperative, a women led and managed initiative that aims to develop a development bank in Malawi.

She has successfully created a successful family business operating nationwide after starting as a small sole trader in her home garage.

she has taken on the leadership role at Business Consult Africa where she was the Managing Director for 8 years from 2000 to 2008.

As a consultant, Towera has undertaken a number of assignments on behalf of clients such as The World Bank, International Finance

Corporattion - Bank, The Gates Foundation, Water for People, Ministry of Agriculture, African Institute of Corporate Initiative, Wildlife Society of Malawi, TraidCraft Uk, Fair Trade Netherlands, Total Land Care, NBS Bank, Concern Universal, Research Into Use, Oxfam and numerous private businesses.

Her work includes value chain analyses, entrepreneurship development, business planning, strategic planning, export trade, public private partnership (PPP) development, fair trade and market research.

Who I am...

I am Towera Jalakasi, married with 3 children, and born in a family of 8 children of 3 boys and 5 girls. I studied Education and majored in Food and Nutrition. I also did fine arts in which I studied how to sculpture, paint and produce ceramics.

After my graduation, in 1991, I taught for a bit at Chichiri secondary school and moved to National seed as a Merchandising Manager in their milling division and progressed into marketing and advertising and finally went into consulting.

I then studied for an Advanced Diploma in Business Counselling and consulting at Dharam Business School in the UK.

This led me into mainstream consulting, locally and internationally, working with various organizations with a focus on enterprise development and working with SME's donors, governments and the private sector.

I know run a company called, Naturals Limited which focuses on natural fruit juices. Our flagship product is baobab juice under the "Khathi Khathi" brand.

How it all began

Since I love to work with my hands, my vision was to do something on my own and not really to "graduate and work". So when I graduated, I planned to venture into a business in fine arts such as producing ceramics of cups, teapots and plates etc. However, I faced challenges because I didn't know exactly where to get the right type of clay and did not have a kiln used to heat the ceramics. I couldn't afford the Kiln, so I literally shelved that dream due to the high capital investment required.

However, I did a bit of clothing and textile business where I imported cloth and made outfits for my customers and was doing it while working elsewhere as a small business, and was more of a side show.

However, as a consultant I had many business ideas but always told myself that "I don't have time to do business as a consultant and even as an employee". I later identified a farm in Neno in Mwanza district where I did irrigated tomato farming since it was near the Lisungwi River. But each time I visited the farm I noticed so much baobab fruit just cast on the ground and simply rotting with people doing nothing with it.

One of the days, I picked the fruit and wondered "can't I make a juice out of this?" So I took the fruit and made juice, just as a try, and took it to church. The reaction I got from the people who tasted it was encouraging. They said "it's nice and it's a unique drink. It's not what we drink every day and we love it!"

So I kept it up and made the juice every time I visited the farm and served it on several occasions including one big occasion at church, called "Friends Sunday" where we invite a lot of people and our friends to church. When I served the juice some people who loved it came to me, more like confronted me, and said "hey your juice is nice, why don't you start selling this juice as a business?" It struck me and made me think that "I am a seasoned consultant providing business development services, so why didn't I think of this".

I told the person that "I'll try" not only to get her off my back but also as a real realization of my untapped potential.

I employed some women from the church and started producing roughly 100 bottles which we sold in offices. My customers came back to me and said 'we love the juice but why can't we find it in shops, why not put it in shops?'

So I thought of responding to this need as well and I improved my packaging a bit to allow for selling in shops. I put it in small shops and true to the concerns, the juice was selling quite fast. But soon enough, the people came back and said "we find it in small shops only why not in PTC?"

PTC (Peoples Trading Centre) shops were a large chain of shops that was prominent at the time. I decided to approach PTC who gave me a checklist of things I needed to do, such as compliance with the

Malawi Bureau of Standards (MBS) requirements, better packaging, supply capacity (considering the vast number of shops), and delivery lead times and so on. I went back to the drawing board and started thinking more like an entrepreneur and decided to develop a business plan. Looking back now, I laugh at myself because as a consultant, I always preach the gospel of "you can't do a business without a business plan" but here I was thinking I could do without one.

Establishing the business

I then increased the capacity of people from 3 women to 8 (of course we are now much more than this) and improved our processes including getting MBS certification and semi-automated our production process to meet demand.

I was only given 1 shop in Blantyre and within a week they product had run out. I approached them and said, the product is not lasting, you need to give us more shops. They initially gave me an additional shop, but the trend was the same, rapid sales and asking for more shops. This trend continued steadily but surely, until we were given access to all their shops in the southern region.

But, not wanting to be left out, our customers told us that "hey we find this juice in Blantyre, so why is it not found in Lilongwe?" this made me do a market research in Lilongwe and contact some outlets in the city. I soon had a small branch in Lilongwe where we rented an office, actually a house from which were operating.

We soon got the interest of donors who wanted to help us improve our capacity and systems and we used their funding for this purpose but also to do a research on the adequacy of Baobab trees and the level of investment that they can justify. We studied the feasibility of establishing a factory in Lilongwe which we later did and then worked on improving the distribution of our product.

We noted that in order to sustain supply in our distribution chain, we needed to engage the first level of our value chain who are the suppliers of the baobab. We engaged about 1,000 collectors in Mwanza,

Neno, Salima and Mangochi and give them supply quota's and supply dates that are in 6 months time.

We would have gone to Mozambique for enough supply and to make us produce for the whole year, but that would be irresponsible of us because we would not be empowering our countrymen and so we decided to first engage the locals in the supply chain. We don't just buy from them we also share our ethos and vision and give them a quota they should meet in 6 months' time. So instead of buying supply outside the country all at once, we have decided to schedule and coordinate the supply network we have in the country. When we want to increase their quota we ask them, also in advance, whether they can meet the supply.

Challenges along the way

Some of the challenges are that we now face a bit of competition, and how we are dealing with this is to do regular market research so we know who is on the market and what we discovered is interesting, that most entrants are "as seasonal as the fruit itself".

When the fruit is in season we have a lot of entrants, and when the season is over, they also disappear. So our strategy is to ensure constant supply of the fruit and we do this by managing our supply chain, buying at the right times and in right quantity, we get the powder, and store enough reserves for "year round" production.

Another strategy is diversification and as a result, we are now venturing into other fruits including mango juice production, and we are utilizing our supply chain of at least 1,000 collectors. We have given them seedlings to grow which will start yielding in 3 years' time and meanwhile we are buying the mango fruit as we produce the juice.

Another strategy is that we are eyeing the flavored drinks market which in itself is not too nutritionally balanced and we want to infuse our flavored drinks with nutrition from baobab and other fruit.

Another worrying trend on the market is the quality of the product itself, resulting in poor taste or even layering and sedimentation of the product when it's on the shelf. What I have done is to bring in my food and nutrition knowledge so that I know for example what heat will do to food or what the cold can do to the chemical makeup and breakdown of the product. This has led me come up with a secret recipe of the various products which takes these factors into account to ensure that both the taste and quality of the product is maintained during its determined shelf life. We have also standardized it in such a way that even though you are new and you join our operations, you will be able to make the same product of similar quality just by following the recipe we have created.

In businesses, challenges do not end, and we continue to face some regarding our distribution channels especially in some private retail chain stores. Of the 4 major chains currently in Malawi, we are now only in Shoprite which is an international chain, but for the local chains we are only in 1 shop and unfortunately are stocking only one of the, more than 4, product lines that we have to offer. Sadly, this is the case when these local retail chains have over 30 outlets each. We hope that this challenge will be overcome through the "Buy Malawi" campaign where the Malawi government is trying to ensure that indigenous products are being merchandised in our local shops.

It is my hope that the retail chains will also have indigenous players, that is, if they can compete fairly in a market that uses unfair and illegitimate business practices to survive.

Other challenges we faced along the way are financing and having a skilled labor force.

Financing is key because it helps to push your vision forward at a much faster rate. We had challenges with the banks because of their need for high-value collateral. So our internal funds were invested into the factory which we can then use, if necessary, as collateral for additional financing. However, what we have noted with the banks is that they don't really move with your vision because they can only give you so much, when you require so much more. I think where I am in 2022, I should have been in 2016, because our levels of financing are inadequate for all the necessary investments of the business. I think I am moving very slowly because of the limited resources I have or can have access to in case I choose to borrow. So we end up growing organically and slowly.

The other concern of skilled labor is equally critical in order to develop quality products and have efficient processes. We invest in training our staff but we have also noted that over time they do not appreciate the value that they have gained through our training investments which results in high labor turnover. And when you are a growing business, sometimes you fail to attract the appropriate talent as we cannot always compete with the market. So keeping the right balance is an issue.

Currently our products lines include three types of baobab fruit juice, bwemba (tamarind) and mango. We also have baobab cosmetic oil extracted from the seed and the remainder of the seed is the baobab cake which we think we can use to produce animal feed as an alternative to soya based animal feed. This cake is good for chicken feed and is currently under research pending introduction to the market.

Looking back at how I grew the business, I started as a sole proprietor but later involved my sister and then grew it to a limited company with her and my children as shareholders. It took a while for everyone to catch the vision but over time we all ran with it. It's more of a family business but the challenge has been to share the passion to the next generation.

I think I managed to inculcate the culture of doing business into them by involving them from the very beginning through asking them to do small tasks, talking about it, seeking their opinions on the taste and quality of the product and so on, and this helped them internalize the vision and grow the need to support it. I think one thing that has encouraged them is seeing how far we have come. We started from a garage and now "here we are!"

My last born child is now helping me with the online marketing of our cosmetics products because that's what he has studied and that's how everyone contributes to the business. In their own little way they bring something to the table.

Hopes for the future

Looking forward we think the cosmetic oil and related products has great online and international potential which we should launch anytime from mid 2022. We are now eyeing the international market for the rest of our products and are already working on improving our branding.

Final words?

I think if you have a vision you should pursue it with all you've got. And when you engage in business go for it as long as there is "potential" to grow. You must however assess yourself and see your strong and weak points. Once you make peace with this, it will inform you of how to progress. You will face challenges but I believe you can always over-come. I also encourage local businesses to build businesses that will last and live after them so they can build something bigger than themselves and not just operate as a sole trader.

Maya Nkoloma

"The tech philanthropist"

Maya Nkoloma is the founder of iMoSyS. iMoSyS exists to provide industry leading responses to socio economic challenges through our expertise in Engineering & Information Technology with the ultimate goal of making life better.

The solutions he has come up with will warm your heart as you discover the philanthropist in him.

Maya holds an MSc in wireless communication and a Master of Technology degree in advanced Information Technology with a specialisation in telecommunications and networking from the International Institute of Information and Technology (I²IT) in Pune, India. Additionally, he obtained a BSc in Electrical Engineering.

Fast facts

Year of Birth   1984

Company   iMoSyS

Countries   Malawi

Education   MSc in wireless communication : University of Sheffield in UK

Master of Technology degree in advanced Information Technology

Major - telecommunications and networking : Institute of Information and Technology (I²IT) Pune, India.

BSc in Electrical Engineering: The Malawi Polytechnic.

Achievements

MoSyS won the "Startup Company of the Year' 2021 by the ICT Association of Malawi, ICTAM on account of the "iTap" project which is an Automated Water Vending Machine that dispenses potable water in rural communities. Another project that contributed to this was the telecom site monitoring systems for the telecommunication industry.

The Vice President of Malawi recognised iMoSyS and its projects as being with a high social impact. This was made as he was giving a public lecture entiltled 'Promoting Digitalisation For Revival OF The SADC Industrial Agenda In The Covid 19 Era' during the 41st Ordinary Summit of SADC Heads of State & Government.

iMoSyS participates in several exhibitions including one for the SADC Industrialisation Week and the ITU Telecoms World Event in Busan, South Korea.

Maya received the prestigious yearly, national innovation award in the field of Science and Technology from Malawi Broadcasting Corporation (MBC). In both 2017 and 2018, he received a global award at ITU Telecom world for promoting innovative ICT solutions with greatest social impact.

iMoSyS partnered with a technology development provider called Azuka and obtained sole distributorship rights of "Sisense BI" in Malawi.

During the Covid 19 pandemic iMoSyS was given a grant to establish a manufacturing facility for the production of face shields at a large scale.

Who am I

I think I can describe myself as a young man who likes to build solutions. For me, it's not just about solving problems, it's that with a little more... I have a focus on applying technology to solve problems. I have a desire to make life better through technology and engineering technical know how. I want to make like better, I want to bring change and I want to see solutions to the problems around us and society at large.

I am married to my lovely wife Nenauthe, and I have 3 boys including a set of twins.

My early days

Born in 1982 in Bvumbwe, my parents were agriculturalists, horticulturists to be specific, at Bvumbwe research station and we later moved to the Natural Resources College in Lilongwe and then the National Botanic Gardens in Zomba where I did my primary education in these two places. And from Zomba Primary School I was selected to Dedza Secondary school. This was quite a feat because I emerged top of the class and was lucky enough to be awarded an admission to this renowned school, especially considering the number of students we have in primary schools. At Zomba primary school we had about 4 streams of the final class meaning there was stiff competition, especially when you think that a single class could have about 100 students, give or take.

After Dedza secondary school I was selected to the The Polytechnic, a constituent collect of the University of Malawi. But we mostly lived in Zomba for a majority of my primary school education and through college. Sadly, I faced a painful experience in my second year when my father died in 2001. It happened at the worst time.... when my siblings were just starting their lives and they could not fill the gap left by my dad. But the most important thing and greatest challenge for my mum was to put us through school. Fortunately, she fought as hard as she could and we all went to school, including myself. And as a family, we helped each other out, deciding and working to support each one of us through college. One of the ways I helped out with the burden was to do something during the holidays. I was working during the holidays and started in the first year of college at Orbit Television, which was owned by my brother. The company was a spin-off from Rays Limited which was a pioneer of satellite television in Malawi and it later became Multichoice Malawi Limited.

Since I worked throughout my college life, I had a special advantage because it was in my field of study and was complimentary by giving me practical work experience. Nonetheless, it was a humble job, because apart from the technical aspects of the job I was also supposed to do basic installations of TV, satellite dishes and aerials. A successful installation meant you really know your job because there were few of us and also we did not have these fancy gadgets, like signal finders of today which make the job easier.

I soon learnt to value financial savings because the savings from my job were used for my personal needs. I had another source of income because I always qualified for the best engineering student awards since I was constantly top of the class. The financial reward that comes with the awards helped me to complement my savings and provide for myself. All these things helped me to survive and do well in college so much so that it was not too apparent that I was an orphan.

The loss of my father was a tough event in my life and it meant I had to stand up and look at how I can almost fend for myself and look for ways of surviving. Perhaps if my father were rich and left us a hefty inheritance I might not have developed the character and sense of independence I have today. It was tough but I basically had to learn to swim.

Anyway, I graduated in 2005 with a degree in electrical engineering and was offered an associate lecturer position, specializing in telecommunications. My head of department at the time was Dr. Gombachika who supported me a lot and put me into research and my research was on the impact of wireless communications or WiFi on the country's medical sector, in collaboration with a certain Italian research institute/laboratory.

We found that technology has a key role in remote healthcare facilities by leveraging the use of wireless technology in medical service delivery. The thesis was that 'if we have facilities with only a medical officer, we can use wireless communications so that more technical expertise is provided via a consultation process to alleviate delays in specialized diagnoses and treatment of patients'. This is helpful to minimize the impact of inadequate skills and knowledge of medical officers in the ground.

The use and application of my tech services posed a unique challenge because on its own it can easily be sidelined due to the plethora of challenges that the country faces. Any government would rather invest in clean water, abundant food, quality education and health services and so on, each government will have its own drive and campaign promises, whether it's the Nsanje cargo port, free agricultural input programs, creating a million jobs, investing in enough roads and so on, and even in the midst of fulfilling those promises, Each government will have to deal with it's fair share of unplanned problems like natural disasters, such as the recent flooding due to the several cyclones that have ravaged the country.

So through my mentorship under Dr. Gombachika, I learnt an important recipe of how to sell technology. I learnt that we have to change our language from 'I am selling tech' to 'I have a solution that can reduce death in rural hospitals by enabling direct specialist support to even the most remote medical facilities'. Now... that's something that the government will understand, so we stopped talking about 'WiFi' but rebranded it in a way that enabled us and the government to be in sync.

This is a recipe I learnt from him (my mentor) and one that I am still using till today, this helps us be in sync with the needs of the current environment of a developing country so our message is now 'we can help you reduce illness and death, you can give clean water, there will be no waterborne illnesses, less cases of tuberculosis' and so on and so forth.

One of the challenges that our country faces is lack of adequate research facilities and I was quite privileged to work with the Italian lab because even our top Malawian institutions don't have the necessary equipment to conduct some of these contemporary technological research. What this did was to give me unique capabilities through very high end technology and facilities that my contemporaries did not have. And from the outside, it apparently looked like I was lagging behind. Because my colleagues were quickly attaining further qualifications beyond the undergraduate and even attained masters degrees. They easily got doctorates while I took my time from 2005 to 2009, busy with my first degree research. This looked so awkward in a highly academic and competitive environment.

However, the same approach I took is taken in places like Germany where you don't rush to a masters or a doctorate degree soon after the first degree graduation. The requirement is to first practice and work in industry and understand the challenges the country faces. The understanding you get forms a basis for a thesis which really solves the problems of society. Similarly, you don't just rush for a PhD soon after a masters, you still have to work for two or three years so that your findings are aligned to societal problems. This is why most of us who have these advanced qualifications have little to no impact because we have rushed the process, without experience, without understanding the problems that really need to be solved, they just don't really know what people go through. And to make matters worse, most will actually be given a topic, that should be studied and the findings of the research will mostly benefit the country they are studying in or the country of the examining body or university.

The fact that others will not be in sync with people's problems is what has contributed to my being a little bit unique because that's the exact challenge I was fortunate enough to overcome.

As I said, it was only in 2009, four years after my graduation that I went for further studies pursuing a masters degree in technology with a specialization in networking and data communications It was called Master of Technology in Information Technology or 'MTech' for short . It was a two year year program in India. It was a lovely experience and very challenging and demanding. It had a focus in programming in various languages and was quite a paradigm shift from my experience of handling wires and so on. So while as engineers we learn programming languages in our first degree, it was more of a side show and not really our cup of tea.

We were given various assignments such as 'do such and such a task using 'C' language, change the number from decimal to binary using '1's and 0's' (As in '01010') and so on'.

In fact I was a little older than my classmates because they were not only younger and fresher, if not sharper, but were extremely competitive. They actually did not use a calculator because in India they believed that the calculator makes you dull. And, as I would be busy with my calculator they would already be doing complex calculations and arrive at the answer. I discovered that because of their large population of at least 1.2bn people, those who find themselves in college are super smart and that's why they could do complex mental calculations. But in spite of these odds I did very well.

On my return in. 2011, I started my tech company called iMoSys. However the real returns started showing around 2016 and 2017, so it takes resilience to not only remain but also to be established and succeed in business.

I later did another 1 year Masters degree in 2015 at Sheffield University, United Kingdom. This was a 'Masters in wireless Technology'.

Setting up the business

Setting up the business was a big mountain to climb since the financial burden was all on my shoulders. I had no one who would fund me to launch into business. However, I decided to come up with a strategy that would build on my life lessons from childhood to university and beyond. And as already said, instead of talking about technology I came up with a strategy to *'solve important national problems in 6 key areas namely, agriculture, water, energy, education, industrialization and health'*. These areas are also aligned to the priority areas of our government for the development of our country. And for example, in the area of water we would approach the water board companies and tell them the reasons why they are failing in certain areas and say 'but if you use our technology you will increase people's access to water'. They would be rather skeptical of course, especially in the absence of a track record and a renowned name. But they would be surprised that we were delivering on our promise. One of the strategies we used is to ensure that we demonstrate the value-add to the business in terms of quantified monetary savings or efficiencies.

One other area we had to look out for is doing clean business and applying and qualifying for necessary business licenses and certifications. That is very important for us to ensure we tick the boxes in procurement processes so we also manage our reputation risk.

As we continue to achieve various milestones in business, there is always that one project that that is close to your heart. And for me it was a project in rural and peri urban communities water access. What we saw was that these communities use central or communal water kiosks. The model has several challenges and prerequisites, for example, if the kiosk operator is not there, for reason of illness or for any other reason, then the community has no water. Or, if he has friends and relatives, he might be tempted to serve it for free, leading to a lot of revenue leakage. And the system, also needs to be maintained by the communities in case of damage and wear and tare those costs need to be managed and revenue generated to cover them.

After appreciating all these costs and challenges, we basically proposed an automation solution to bring in accountability, solve revenue leakage and ensure virtually 24/7, round the clock access to water and essentially cut off the human limitations of the system, it was also also powered by solar. After installing the solution at a site in Lilongwe I asked one of my guys to send me a video of the install so I could see how well it's working.

By the time I finished watching the video, I discovered that it was on my Polytechnic class WhatsApp group, then it was on my family group, then on a church group and it went viral across the world, literally across the world!

The video showed how ecstatic a woman was when she was able to use her card to simply swipe on the machine and it automatically dispensed water. It was like magic and as soon as the watered gushed out she started screaming and saying 'oh things have changed in Ntchesi, now it's more advanced! Let me call my momma and tell her things have changed'. All in vernacular of course! She was ululating and dancing and clapping and jumping up and down with bystanders sharing in her contagious joy. The joy and jubilation of this woman and many others like her, just make it all worth it. It reminds me we are doing something worthwhile.

The other project that's close to my heart is a TB treatment tracking and compliance program called 'eHealth Management System'. As you might be aware it is very critical for people to be on the full treatment course of TB. And we follow and manage the system from cradle to grave. That means we start from tracking the samples in and from at least 20 health facilities across the country, we get data of samples collected for testing and we follow them through to delivery and testing. We get a red flag if any sample is not delivered. And, in the case of TB, the challenge of treatment is that of defaulters. Patients are not given all their medicine at once and they have to come to the hospital at intervals. They get reminders, for example, 'that tomorrow you have a scheduled hospital visit'. And if they don't pitch up, the system will alert health personnel and volunteers who will then follow them up to ensure they finish their treatment. The same volunteers are the ones who help even in collection of TB samples and they really ensure that this is tested speedily because the sample has to be collected and tested within 7 days of collection.

The solutions we bring to the Malawi environment can easily be replicated across the country because the Southern and wider Africa region shares similar challenges meaning it is possible to scale these solutions across borders.

Hopes for the future

My hopes for the future are that we can continue to identify important problems in society. To continue using tech to solve these problems and make life easier for society. With some effort, we should be able to scale these solutions not only from small communities but to the country at large and also across our borders where problems are similar to our own.

Moffat Ngalande FCCA, CA (Mw), CGEIT, BAcc. is a Fellow of the Association of Certified chartered Accountant, a Chartered Accountant and licensed
practicing auditor with the Malawi Accountants Board and the Institute of
Chartered Accountants in Malawi (ICAM). He is Certified in the Governance
of Enterprise IT (CGEIT) and holds a bachelor's degree in Accounting.

He is a Partner of AuditConsult, A correspondent firm of RSM International, in Audit, Tax and Advisory and was previously an Associate Director
of PwC.

In September 2022, he was elected as President of the Institute of Chartered
Accountants in Malawi (ICAM) having ably served as the Vice President of
ICAM from year 2020 through 2022. Until 2022 he was the Chairperson of
the Technical Standards Committee of ICAM, leading the provision of key
guidance on various matters affecting the accountancy profession in Malawi.

He is involved with the Dynamic Leaders and Gate Keepers Forum where
he leads the "Business Gate" of the Forum and is also an ambassador of the
Global Leadership Network in Malawi.

He has authored serval bestselling titles, including Taxation in Malawi and
enjoys mentoring the youth in various forums.